FABULOUS
Feathers & Fillers

DESIGN & MACHINE QUILTING TECHNIQUES

SUE NICKELS

 American Quilter's Society

P.O. Box 3290 • Paducah, KY 42002-3290
Fax 270-898-1173 • e-mail: orders@AQSquilt.com

Located in Paducah, Kentucky, the American Quilter's Society (AQS) is dedicated to promoting the accomplishments of today's quilters. Through its publications and events, AQS strives to honor today's quiltmakers and their work and to inspire future creativity and innovation in quiltmaking.

EXECUTIVE BOOK EDITOR: ANDI MILAM REYNOLDS
BOOK EDITOR: KATHY DAVIS
GRAPHIC DESIGN: ELAINE WILSON
COVER DESIGN: MICHAEL BUCKINGHAM
QUILT PHOTOGRAPHY: CHARLES R. LYNCH

Additional copies of this book may be ordered from the American Quilter's Society, PO Box 3290, Paducah, KY 42002-3290, or online at www.AmericanQuilter.com.

Text © 2013, Author, Sue Nickels
Artwork © 2013, American Quilter's Society

American Quilter's Society
P.O. Box 3290 • Paducah, KY 42002-3290
Fax 270-898-1173 • e-mail: orders@AQSquilt.com

Library of Congress Control Number: 2013932236

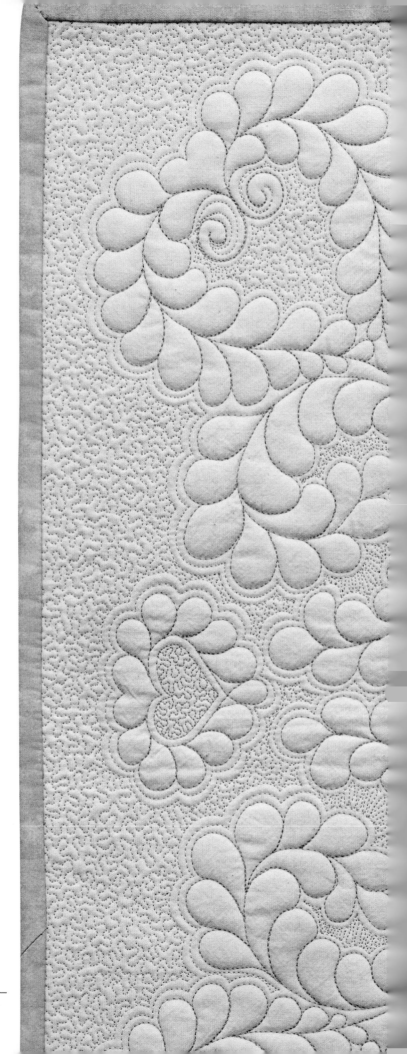

title page: PROJECT SIX: LEMON SORBET, detail, full quilt on page 100

opposite: PROJECT TWO: MINT JULEP, detail, full quilt on page 92

Dedication

I would like to dedicate this book to my good friend Gwen Marston. I first met Gwen while attending her retreat on Beaver Island in 1986. I was a fairly new quilter and eager to learn everything about quilting. Gwen's easy-going approach to quiltmaking was so refreshing! I attended Gwen's retreats for many years after that and this is where I fell in love with the feather design. I learned to draw beautiful feathers with her guidance. This book would not exist if not for Gwen and her techniques. I also thank Gwen for her encouragement to try my hand at writing and also teaching machine quilting and machine-appliqué techniques. Gwen has been a mentor to me and my sister, Pat Holly. We have achieved more success with our quilting than we could have ever imagined thanks to Gwen's support and encouragement. Thank you, Gwen, for passing along your passion for quilting and for being a friend for life!

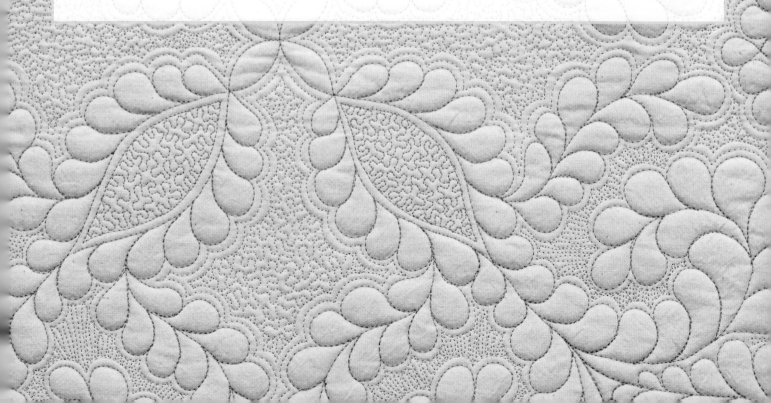

Acknowledgments

◇◇◇

I would like to thank the following people who have helped me throughout the process of writing this book. I could not have done it without their support.

To my AQS editors, Andi Reynolds and Kathy Davis, thank you for your confidence in my skills, your patience, and guidance.

To the American Quilter's Society family, thank you for your continued support of quiltmakers and your love of quilting.

To BERNINA of America, thank you for the generous use of my BERNINA sewing machines. They make machine quilting easy and enjoyable. A special thanks to Jeanne Delpit whose enthusiasm and happy spirit are an inspiration!

To the Ann Arbor Sewing Center, my local quilt shop and BERNINA dealer, for their support and for the beautiful fabrics used in many of the small projects in this book. Thanks Doni and Kris!

To Ricky Tims, thank you for your beautiful rhapsody hand-dyed fabric used in the project "Mint Julep."

To my sister, Pat Holly, thank you for your expertise, support, and advice throughout the writing of this book.

To my family, thanks to Tim, Ashley, Jessi, Ryan, Stella, and Grandma GG for being my biggest fans!

left: PROJECT THREE: ORANGE SHERBET, detail, full quilt on page 94

Contents

Introduction

This is my second book on machine quilting. I wasn't sure I wanted to write another; *Machine Quilting: A Primer of Techniques* has been very successful. It is thorough and teaches my techniques nicely.

I have machine quilted since 1987 and have taught since the early 1990s. I have seen a huge shift in the popularity of machine quilting over those years. When I first started, very few quilts were machine quilted. In fact, most traditional quilters frowned on the thought of using the machine for quilting. "It's not really a quilt if it has been machine quilted" was a comment that I often heard.

The sewing machine companies now offer many features to make machine quilting easier so it has become popular. Some of the features that help include: larger arm area for the bulk of the quilt, varied darning foot options, good cabinets with room for the quilt to be supported, and more. It has been rewarding to see the workmanship in machine quilting continue to become better and more refined.

There are many different ways to approach machine quilting. I do my quilting on my home sewing machine which is a standard size and I have been very successful. I also have a machine that has a larger arm area; this makes it nice for larger quilts.

Many quilters machine quilt beautifully on long-arm machines; this is not just for business any more. There are machines in between the long-arm and home machines that offer more arm room and can fit easily at home. These mid-arm machines offer many great features and good results. How lucky we are to have so many choices available as machine quilters.

With so many options available, I thought I would run out of students interested in machine quilting on the home sewing machine. It has been just the opposite and my machine-quilting classes remain extremely popular! I believe that my students want to be successful at machine quilting their own quilts and the machine they have is a home sewing machine. That is good news for me, because I love to teach machine quilting.

I have used feathers as a quilting motif since I was a hand quilter. When I discovered I could free-motion machine quilt feathers, I knew I could be a machine quilter. Then I discovered from my friend Gwen Marston I could design my own feathers to be any size, shape, or style, and fit in any area on my quilt top!

opposite: TEA AT TENBY, a collaborative quilt made by the author and her sister, Pat Holly. This quilt is not patterned in this book.

I taught machine-quilted feathers for many years and had a small section on stitching feathers in my first book. I have also taught how I draw feathers over the years and have been asked if I would write my technique for designing feathers. It wasn't until I started working with the wholecloth feather concept that I felt I was creating something unique and my own original idea.

The first quilt I used the wholecloth quadrant format for a feather design was TEA AT TENBY, page 6, a collaborative quilt made by my sister, Pat Holly, and me. It has been exhibited in many shows and won some very nice awards, including Best of Show at the 2009 Birmingham Festival of Quilts in England.

Pat designed and made the beautiful appliqué top with a large border area that would look great with intricate quilting. We had collaborated on many quilts in the past and shared in the design and appliqué process. TEA AT TENBY was a great way to make a collaborative quilt again and I became the machine quilter for this project.

I looked at many books of antique quilts that had beautiful feather designs. I wanted something unique and intricate. I also looked at Pat's books on antique textiles and found a book on antique woven coverlets. There was an interesting coverlet design that looked feather-like. I used this for my inspiration and designed the feather motif for TEA AT TENBY. I used a thin cream-colored cotton thread and accented some areas with a gold-colored silk thread. The result—an intricately shaded wholecloth feather-type motif. I was on my path to a whole new way of designing unique feathers.

Now I have something new to offer quilters. With Gwen's blessing to write this book, I am excited to present you with techniques you can use for your next quilt project!

I will discuss the supplies I use with my design techniques and machine-quilting methods and will share how I design feathers, from basics to wholecloth concepts. I will then cover machine-quilting techniques for feathers and fillers.

I feel it is really important to give quilters the techniques to work on real quilts, so we will cover marking, basting, and managing the actual quilt at the home sewing machine. I will provide you with both practice sessions and small wholecloth projects. I hope you enjoy my second machine-quilting book!

Fondly,

Sue Nickels

opposite: This little quilt was made by Gwen Marston. She explains, "I saw the heart-shaped feathers on the border of an early Caesar's Crown quilt in the Shelburne collection. I adapted the border design for the heart-shaped feather wreaths in the plain blocks."

SECTION ONE: *Supplies*

This section of the book will discuss the supplies I use to design feathers, mark and baste the actual quilt, and free-motion quilt feathers and fillers. Refer to the products page for a list of specific brands I use.

Design Supplies

Paper

Use either white copy paper or heavier artist drawing paper for making the feather spine patterns. These are sold in art and office supply stores.

Fig. 1. Paper, large pad paper, tracing paper, pencils, pens, rulers, and a compass

Tracing Paper

Architect or engineering sketch paper is perfect for designing feathers. This is an inexpensive, lightweight tracing paper sold on a 50-yard roll in 12", 18", 24", and 36" widths. It is sold at art supply and campus book stores that have architecture or engineering programs. It can also be purchased online.

Pencils

Sharp lead pencils are used for designing and drawing on paper.

Pens

Black fine-point markers are used to draw feather motifs on paper. This drawing is used as a pattern to place under the quilt top for marking.

Rulers

Quilters' rulers, sold at quilt shops, are used for measuring and drawing straight lines. Metal drafting-type rulers, sold at art and office supply stores, can also be used and are very accurate.

Compass

A good quality compass can be used in the design process. I use one that locks to the specific size needed. These can be purchased at office supply and art stores. Cheap compasses don't stay locked and make it harder to achieve accuracy.

Marking Supplies

Pencils

For the methods used in this book, it is necessary to mark the feathers on the quilt top before basting. I use a soft, chalk-based pencil which draws easily on fabric, leaves a visible line, and is easy to remove. The silver pencil usually works well but if it does not show on the fabric, try white. Use a manual pencil sharpener to sharpen the pencil to a short point. If the point is long, it will break easily.

I recommend testing any marking products carefully to make sure the marks come off completely. Do not iron your top after it has been marked because the heat might set the marks and make them harder to remove.

Tracing Paper

Tracing paper is used to sketch quilting designs to fit on a specific area. I lay the paper over the quilt top and lightly draw my designs.

Light Box

A light box is used when marking complex quilting designs on dark or busy fabrics. Inexpensive ones are available at quilt shops and craft supply stores. You can create your own light box by placing a light underneath a clear acrylic sewing machine extension table. A light box is a wonderful tool for quilting.

Batting

There are many battings available. Always buy good quality and consider the look you want for your finished quilt, as well as the purpose. When quilting feathers and fillers, I like my batting to have some loftiness. The feathers will show nicely as dimension is created by the filler stitching that surrounds the feather.

I like cotton-blend batting for this reason. It has the nice qualities of cotton batting and the little bit of polyester gives a loftier appearance. 100% cotton can be very flat and this dimensional effect will not happen. I don't use super lofty 100% polyester battings because they are harder to machine quilt. There are other types of batting available, including wool, silk, bamboo, and blends.

Open your batting and let it breathe before using it in your quilt to allow any wrinkles or

Fig. 2. Marking pencils, light box, and tracing paper over a quilt top

---

folds to relax before basting. Test the batting with the fabric and threads you are using in the quilt; it is important to know what the finished result will be before you baste and start quilting, only to realize you aren't happy with the look. Always read the instructions for the batting to know how far apart to quilt and if it is recommended to pretreat or prewash.

Cotton Batting

100% cotton gives a flatter look to your quilt. It packages nicely and is easy to handle. This batting may require closer and heavier quilting.

Cotton-blend Batting

There are many types and brands of cotton-blend battings. I use an 80% cotton/20% polyester batting. It is a good choice for machine quilting because it handles much like 100% cotton but the polyester makes the batting loftier and the quilting designs will show nicely. This is my favorite batting for quilting feathers and fillers. Refer to the instructions on the package for pretreating.

Polyester Batting

There are numerous polyester battings available. Most have a loftier appearance than cotton and have a more slippery surface which needs to be basted closely to keep it from shifting when quilting. Polyester is harder to package at the sewing machine. Clips can be used to keep the quilt from unrolling. Use dark polyester battings when quilting dark fabrics to avoid noticeable bearding.

Wool Batting

This is a popular batting for machine quilting. It looks and acts like polyester batting when quilted, very lofty, and the quilting designs show beautifully. Wool is a natural fiber which makes it a desirable choice and is warm and breathable.

Silk Batting

Silk makes a beautiful lightweight batting. The brand I have used is a blend that has some polyester added. Because of its natural ability to breathe, silk is an excellent choice for airy, lightweight quilts. It machine quilts magnificently. It has specific and careful washing instructions and has some shrinkage.

Fabric

100% cotton fabric is used for the projects in this book. Always use good quality fabrics. These can be found at your local quilt shop. Wash fabrics for projects that will be laundered after they are completed. 100% cotton fabric shrinks slightly when washed, so it is better to do this before using the fabric in your project. Testing fabrics for running or bleeding is a good idea. Use a product that will set the dyes in fabrics, if needed. See Section Five for information on fabric selection.

Other fabrics can be used for your quilt project. Silks, blends, wool, and many others have been used successfully. Practice first to see if the results are good.

Basting Supplies

An important step to successful machine quilting is to have a well-basted quilt. There are many options for basting. Take time to do a good job, whichever method you choose. I like to baste using safety pins. See Section Five for my basting technique.

Safety Pins

Brass or nickel-plated safety pins in size 1 are used for basting the layers of the quilt. I also like the curved-style safety pins. Very small or very large safety pins can be harder to use. Insert the pins about every 3". A large supply of safety pins is needed for a large quilt. A safety pin closer is a great tool to help close the pins once they are inserted in the quilt layers.

Basting Spray Adhesive

This is a popular way to quickly baste a quilt. It works great on smaller projects, but safety pins may also be required on larger quilts to help secure the layers. The spray contains chemicals that may be harmful, so use it in a well-ventilated area.

Fusible Batting

These cotton and polyester battings can be ironed to baste the layers of the quilt.

Thread Basting

Thread is another basting option. This is not my favorite as I found the darning foot can get caught on the basting threads. These can be hard to remove after they have been stitched over. There are wash-out threads that can be used and would solve that problem.

Free-motion Quilting Supplies
Curved-tip Spring-action Scissors

These special scissors, or snips, are great for cutting the thread ends at the surface of the quilt. Because they are curved, there is never a risk of clipping the fabric. The snips are spring-operated, which means you don't have to put your fingers in the holes of scissor handles. I also use these snips for taking stitches out.

Thread Stand and Auxiliary Guide

Use a thread stand for cone-shaped or big heavy thread spools that won't fit on horizontal or vertical spool pins. An auxiliary guide brings the thread from the thread stand to the exact point on the machine where it should be threaded. Some machines have auxiliary guides, but if yours does not, just use a safety pin taped

Fig. 3. Safety pins, safety pin closer, and basting spray

upside down to the back of the machine or an empty bobbin on the spool pin, and thread through the small hole on each device.

Rubber Glove Fingers

I started machine quilting long before there were products on the market specifically designed for the machine quilter. Right away, I realized it would be helpful to have something on my fingers to easily control and move the quilt when free-motion quilting. When I thought to use my kitchen dishwashing rubber gloves, there was an immediate improvement in my ability to control the stitches. After about five minutes, my hands were sweating uncomfortably, so I cut the fingers off the gloves,

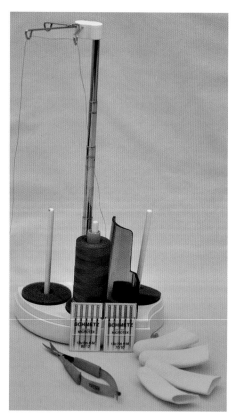

Fig. 4. Sewing machine needles, curved scissors, thread stand, and rubber glove fingers

placed them on the first two fingers of each hand, and have used them ever since.

Now there are many products on the market for this, but I have found the rubber glove fingers give me the best traction or grip, which is important in free-motion quilting. If you have a light touch on the quilt and can still move it easily, the result is smoother, more even stitches. When you don't have enough traction or grip, the tendency is to push harder on the quilt, which results in jerky, uneven stitches.

You may need to use a size smaller glove than you use for dishwashing. The fingers should fit snugly, so they won't fall off while wearing them. Cut the fingers off at the base of the glove; if they are too short they will fall off.

Use the better quality rubber gloves, as they have more grippers. Splurge and buy the best! When the gloves first come out the package, they have a powder on them. Run the gloves under water first to get this powder off.

Sewing Machine

Any type of sewing machine can be used for free-motion quilting. Some machines make the job easier by having convenient features such as feed dogs that can be lowered, a needle-stopping down option, good foot pedal control of the sewing speed, and a large worktable surface. Some have large arm areas for working on larger quilt projects with greater ease. Use the best machine you can afford. It is your essential tool for machine quilting and you should be comfortable with it. Keep it in good working order by having it cleaned and oiled regularly.

Walking Foot

This important foot is used for straight-line quilting. It is also called an even-feed foot. Some machines have a built-in walking foot option. This foot acts like a top set of feed dogs, feeding all three layers of the quilt evenly to prevent puckering and shifting. For better visibility, an open-toe sole plate is available for some walking feet. We will not be using this foot for the small projects, but will use it for anchoring straight lines on larger projects.

Darning Foot

This is essential for free-motion quilting. For this technique the feed dogs are lowered or covered. The darning foot moves up and down slightly and allows the quilt to move freely while keeping it smooth and flat. Free-motion quilting feels different from regular sewing and it takes practice to achieve success. There are different styles of darning feet and each machine brand has its own specific foot. There are open- and closed-toe variations. I prefer the open-toe version as it gives good visibility for seeing marked designs such as feathers. Some machine brands refer to these as freehand-embroidery or freehand-quilting feet. I call the foot I use for free-motion quilting a traditional darning foot.

A new darning foot variation is the BERNINA® Stitch Regulator (BSR). This foot for specific BERNINA models is a darning foot which has a sensor that reads how fast or slow you are moving the quilt and it matches the sewing speed to create consistent stitch length in free-motion quilting. I refer to this as training wheels for the free-motion quilter and it can be helpful, especially for beginners.

Please note—this book is written using a traditional darning foot, not the BSR. Refer to your dealer for specific information on how to use the BSR successfully.

Straight-Stitch Throat Plate

Sewing machines come with a zigzag throat plate that allows zigzag and decorative stitches to be used. This plate has a large oval opening for the machine to do these stitches. When free-motion quilting, the layers may get pushed down into the opening, resulting in poor tension. By changing to a straight-stitch throat plate, which has a single hole for the opening, the quilt lies taut across the opening and a better stitch is made. Remember to only do a straight stitch, no zigzag stitching, with this throat plate.

Fig. 5. Walking foot, darning foot, BSR foot, and straight-stitch throat plate

---

Thread

Your choice of thread is very important. Educate yourself on the varieties of thread available and only use good quality. Thread makes a big difference in the success of your machine quilting. Cheap or poorly-made thread causes problems such as frequent breakage, uneven tension, and skipped stitches. Personal preference is one of the most important reasons to choose a thread.

I use threads that I like how they look and feel in my quilt project. We have many choices, including 100% cotton, polyester, silk, and others. It can be confusing to decide which thread to use. I use certain brands because my local quilt shop carries them, making it easy for me to replenish them. Many brands will work successfully for free-motion quilting and some are available online.

Thread Weights and Plies

There are important factors for choosing a particular thread for a quilt project. Cotton threads typically indicate a weight and sometimes a ply. For instance, the thread might say 50/3 on the label. This means the weight is 50 and it has three plies (three strands twisted together to make the thread). The higher the number (50), the thinner the thread will be and the lower the number, the thicker the thread will be. This also can be an indication of the strength of cotton thread. I refer to a 50/3 cotton thread as an average-weight and average-strength thread. I have used it for piecing, appliqué, and machine quilting. A cotton thread that is 40/3 is a thicker thread and will be stronger. A cotton

thread that is 60/2 will be a thinner thread and is slightly weaker.

How the quilt will be used can determine what thread you will choose. When making a utilitarian quilt that will get used often, washed frequently, and minimally quilted, using a 40/3 cotton will be a good choice. However, a quilt that is quilted heavily with feathers and fillers, using a thinner thread like a 60/2 cotton would be appropriate. A favorite cotton thread of mine is the 50/2 thread. These have the strength of a 50-weight but are slightly thinner because they are two-ply threads.

The thinner the thread, the more it sinks down into the fibers of the fabric and becomes less visible. The thicker the thread, the more it sits up on the fabric and is visible and decorative. In stitching traditional feathers, there is an area of re-stitching. A slightly thinner thread makes this area less visible. When stitching a filler, like traditional stipple quilting, a thinner thread is a nice choice because the stitching will become background and will not be highly visible.

Polyester threads typically don't have a weight indication. These are strong threads, often feel thinner, and are available in beautiful vibrant colors.

Thread Color

The color of the thread is also important. When using a high-contrast thread color, the stitching is very noticeable. If you are new to free-motion quilting and your stitches are not as smooth and consistent as they will be when you have more experience, choose a matching color thread. It will be more forgiving!

Thread Spools

Proper threading of your machine is also important. A general rule is that cross-wound spools should be threaded on a horizontal spool pin, and straight-wound or stacked spools should be threaded on a vertical spool pin. The thread should always come off of the spool easily and go through the tension area evenly. Threads on big, heavy spools or on cone-shaped spools may need to be threaded off of the machine using an auxiliary thread guide and a thread spool stand.

A great website that answers many questions you may have about thread is: **www. Superiorthreads.com**

Thread Testing

I make a small quilt sandwich, about 12" square, pieced with the most prominent fabrics used for my top and the same batting and backing. I then test the threads I want to use to make sure I am happy with the weight, color, and type of thread. I can also check to make sure my thread tension is perfect before quilting my real quilt project.

I like to have the same or similar color thread in both the top and the bobbin. If you have a high contrast thread combination, you will occasionally see top threads show on the back or bobbin threads pop up to the top. I am very careful when choosing my backing fabric. I try to find a busy print that has the same colors used

in the quilt top. This way I can use the same color thread on the top and in the bobbin.

Thread Tension

When talking about threads it is important to discuss thread-tension adjustment. It is very easy to adjust top tension and is done depending on your thread combinations. I often use different weight threads for top and bobbin. This can cause the tension to be imperfect.

If you see bobbin threads showing on the top, loosen your top tension by changing the top tension to a lower number–3 or 2. If you see top threads showing on the back, tighten your top tension by increasing the top tension to a higher number–5 or 6. Even tension on a machine is usually a setting of 4.

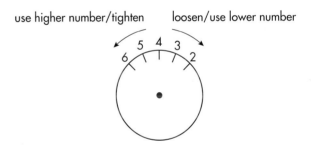

Fig. 6. Top tension adjustment. To tighten, use higher number. To loosen, use lower number.

I rarely need to adjust the bobbin tension because I use very traditional threads and these don't often cause bobbin-tension problems. If you are using very heavy or very thin threads in your bobbin you may need to adjust the tension on the bobbin case. I would recommend a separate bobbin case if this needs to be done often. Talk to your machine dealer for instructions on doing this adjustment.

Thread Types

Descriptions of the various thread types I use successfully for free-motion quilting are listed below. Please note that there are many other thread types available that can be used for home machine quilting. The resources page has some specific brands I like.

Invisible Thread

Also called monofilament, this thread comes in a few varieties. Invisible nylon thread, .004-weight, is usually on a cone-shaped spool. Invisible polyester thread is on a regular spool. When using this thread on the top, I use a 50-weight, 100% cotton thread in the bobbin. Invisible thread may need to be placed on a thread stand. It is very fine and needs to go into the tension area without any pulling. The traditional spool pins can cause this problem. The top tension often needs to be loosened when using these fine threads.

Invisible thread is heat-sensitive. If ironing, turn the iron to the appropriate setting for nylon or polyester fabric. I also use a pressing cloth to be extra safe. Invisible thread can be helpful for beginning machine quilters as it is a thin, clear thread that is forgiving because the stitches are less visible.

Cotton Thread

Always use good quality cotton threads. Look for descriptions like long staple and extra-long staple. Cotton threads are mercerized to help improve luster and strength and are made to have minimal shrinkage. The better ones have less lint, but all cotton threads create some lint that will build up in the bobbin area. Clean and oil the bobbin area frequently.

The following is a description of various cotton threads that I have used to machine quilt.

◆ 50-weight/3-ply Thread

This is an average-weight thread and is a nice choice for quilting, piecing, and appliqué for beginners and intermediate-level quilters. There are quite a few good quality brands.

◆ 50-weight/2-ply Thread

This is another average-weight thread. Because it is 2-ply, it is thinner and is a perfect choice for machine quilting feathers and fillers. It is my favorite thread to use in the bobbin when I sew with 50/3 and 40/3 cotton threads.

◆ 40-weight/3-ply Thread

This heavier thread will be more visible on the fabric. I use this thread when I want a more decorative look. I would not use it for fillers that are closely stitched. I have used it for feathers and larger stipple variations.

◆ 60-weight/2-ply Thread

This is a fine embroidery-weight thread which can be used for machine quilting. It is intended for machine-embroidery techniques where the thread builds up. This is a weaker thread and should only be used for dense free-motion quilting. It is perfect for the small, close fillers that are sometimes referred to as micro-stipple and are used to surround feathers.

Polyester Thread

There are numerous brands of polyester threads available. They come in vibrant and intense colors which make them a great choice for machine quilting. These threads are strong, long-lasting, available in different thicknesses, and can be highly visible or less visible depending on the color and thickness selected.

Silk Thread (100-weight)

This is a beautiful, thin, and very strong thread. It can be used for machine quilting, and is a great choice for small feathers and detailed fillers. It comes in many beautiful colors and heirloom-style machine quilters use silk thread with great results. Its only drawback is that it is more expensive than other threads used for machine quilting.

Decorative Thread

A decorative thread is any thread that contrasts with the quilt fabric. These include cotton in contrasting colors, variegated, metallic, rayon, and acrylic threads. There are many others, with new threads becoming available all the time. To use decorative threads, you must be confident with your machine-quilting skills and have good stitch control. Some decorative threads can be difficult to thread on the machine because of the variety of ways they are packaged on the spool. These threads work best when threaded off the machine, utilizing a thread stand and auxiliary guide.

Fig. 7. Variety of threads used for machine quilting

Needles

Choosing the right machine needle is important. The best needle for a new project is a new one. A needle should be changed after 6–7 hours of stitching. This may seem often; however, a dull needle or one with a burr causes problems such as skipped stitches and uneven tension.

I have always considered two things when choosing a needle. The first is the type of needle which is selected to match the type of fabric being stitched on. We typically use 100% cotton, a lightweight woven fabric, for our quilting projects. It is recommended that a sharper needle be used for these fabrics. There are a few needles that have a sharper point. These include a sharp (sometimes called a Microtex Sharp), a top stitch, and a quilting needle. My favorite machine needle is the sharp. Other machine quilters have had good results with a top stitch as well as a quilting needle.

The second thing to consider is the size of the needle. I select the size in relationship to the weight of the thread. Needle size is indicated by numbers such as 80/12. The 80 is for the European numbering system and the 12 is for the US numbering system. The higher the number on the needle, the larger it is. I consider the 80/12 needle an average size and use it with average-weight threads. If the threads are thicker, I use a larger needle; if the thread is thinner I use a smaller needle.

Here is a list that shows the needle size and the different weight threads:

- 90/14   40/3 cotton thread
    40-weight decorative thread

- 80/12   50/3 cotton thread

- 70/10   50/2 cotton thread
    60/2 cotton thread

- 60/8   100-weight silk
    .004 Invisible threads

If the thread is breaking at the eye of the needle, the eye might too small for the weight (thickness) of the thread. Switch to a larger needle.

There are many needles types that can work for machine quilting. There is not just one perfect needle and you will get many different opinions. I have made my choice after many years of experience and base this on the type of fabric I stitch on and the weight of thread I am using.

Sewing Room

A well-planned sewing room is helpful for successful machine quilting. The following is a description of my sewing room, which hopefully will give you great ideas to set up your sewing space for easier machine quilting.

My sewing machine is at table height, which means it is dropped down into the table. My extension table is the entire sewing table. This allows my quilt to be supported at all times without pulling, dragging, or getting caught anywhere. A large surface area for quilting is important.

Many sewing machine cabinets are now designed with these features. I had a table custom made to fit my workspace. If you can't have a custom-made table or a cabinet specifically for machine quilting, try finding a large acrylic table that will fit your machine and extend your work surface when setting the machine on a table

Fig. 8. Sue's sewing table

My sewing table is deep behind the machine. As the bulk of the quilt moves behind the machine, it doesn't drop off the table or stop at a wall. My table is about 6 feet deep and 3½ feet wide. The machine is at the very front and slightly to the right of the table because more room is needed on the left side to support the bulk of the quilt.

When working at the front of the quilt, I place the quilt over my left shoulder and use an ironing board behind my sewing chair to support the weight of the quilt. I never support the quilt with my body, which helps to eliminate a sore back and shoulders, even when working on large projects. I use an adjustable chair that allows me to easily adjust the height to sit at a perfect position at the machine. With shoulders relaxed, the area from your fingers on the quilt to your bent elbow should be parallel with the floor. Scrunched shoulders can cause neck and shoulder stiffness. Sitting straight in the chair allows me to be close to the machine for good visibility and to support the quilt on my chest and over my shoulder. Don't allow the quilt to drop into your lap as this causes pull or drag and makes it hard to move the quilt easily for free-motion quilting.

Good lighting is an important consideration. If you can't see what you are quilting, you can't quilt very well. I have overhead lighting and a bright tabletop light that is positioned to the right front side of the machine. This light shines brightly on the marked designs I am stitching.

If you can't redesign your sewing room right away, there are many ways to improvise and still have a nice work area. When I first started machine quilting, I placed my machine at the long end of my dining room table. I used old phone books as my extension table. I sat on three pillows to reach the right height and used a floor lamp over my shoulder for lighting. I am happier now with my own customized work space, but I made some pretty nice quilts even in the early days!

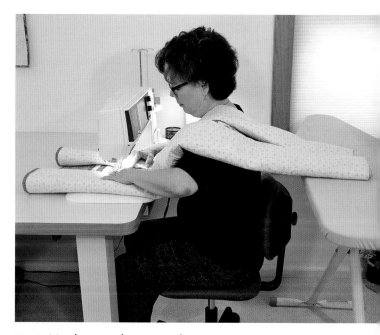

Fig. 9. Machine quilting a quilt

SECTION TWO:

Designing Feathers

The groundwork for my method of drawing feathers was taught by my dear friend and fellow quilt teacher, Gwen Marston, at her Beaver Island Quilt Retreats. I attended her retreats in northern Michigan for many years, beginning in the fall of 1986.

I have always loved the feather as a quilting motif and was thrilled to discover that it is not hard to draw your own original designs. This method does not use a tool or template. You can create your own unique feathers and not be limited by someone else's idea of what one looks like. Everyone will have their own signature style. Starting with the basic feather unit and simple practice exercises, you will be drawing beautiful feathers in no time!

There are two different ways I approach marking feathers on the quilt top. For simple feathers I create a pattern for the center spine. This pattern is used to draw the center spine directly on the fabric. The feathers are then drawn freehand directly on quilt top.

When the feather design becomes more complicated, wholecloth feathers for example, I draw the complete design on paper, lay it under the quilt top to trace onto the fabric, and then free-motion quilt the marked design. I mark the entire quilt top before layering and basting it.

Fig. 1. Simple Feather

Let's learn to design beautiful feathers with ease!

Drawing Simple Feathers

We will break the simple feather shown here into two parts. The first part drawn is the center spine which can be anything but the most common is a curved line. The second part is the basic feather unit. This is drawn on the top and bottom of the spine to make a traditional feather (fig. 1). Feathers drawn on a curved line are seen most often on borders of quilts.

For a feathered wreath, the spine is a circle. For a feathered heart, the spine is a heart. These motifs can be used in various places on a quilt.

We will start drawing feathers using a straight line for the spine. This is the easiest way to see the structure of the basic feather unit. Start by tracing my feather. This is how I see and draw feathers. After you are familiar with drawing the feathers, you can create your signature style!

Practice First

Read this section before starting to draw. Start by placing a piece of paper on top of my practice feather (fig. 2).

With a sharp pencil trace it three times, starting with the spine, then the top row of feathers, and finish with the bottom row.

The basic feather unit looks like half of a heart. For this practice feather, we are drawing the right side of the heart. Begin at the inside point of the feather unit (half-heart) and draw around to meet the spine. Do this in the same order when working on the bottom row. It may seem awkward, but after practice you will draw a more perfect feather.

Draw slowly, take your time, and be consistent. This repetitive exercise will be your foundation for drawing freehand feathers. When learning how to draw feathers, it is important to have top and bottom guidelines to keep the height consistent. Without guidelines, the feather height may get shorter or higher. Eventually you will not need these guidelines.

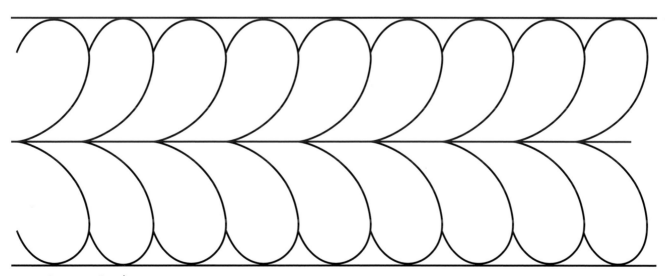

Fig. 2. Practice Feather

Fig. 3. Drawing feathers horizontally

Draw feathers horizontally on your paper, as you would write on paper, working from left to right (fig. 3). This will make it easier to understand and this is how it will be marked on the quilt top most times.

If you are left-handed, try turning the feather pattern upside down. Then work from the right to left, so the feathers are always building on the previous basic feather unit drawn.

There are important rules to follow when drawing the basic feather unit (fig. 4).

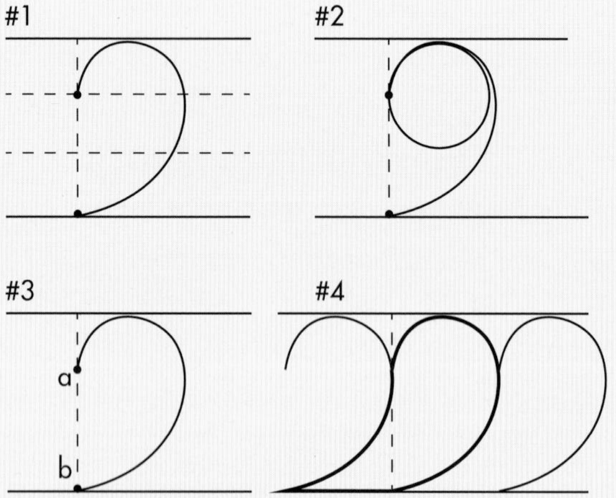

Fig. 4. Basic feather unit

Rule #1: Start ⅓ from the guideline to the center spine.

Rule #2: Shape of feather should be round and consistent.

Rule #3: Starting point a to ending point b—should be perpendicular to the spine.

Rule #4: Keep the teardrop shape of a complete feather.

Rule #1

Start drawing the feather at the inside point of the basic feather unit (half of heart). The starting point should be ⅓ of the way down from the top guideline to the spine. When drawing the bottom feather, the starting point is ⅓ of the way up from the bottom guideline to the spine.

When starting the basic feather unit too close to the guideline, the feathers can look stacked (fig. 5). To correct this, start a little further in from the guideline, closer to the spine.

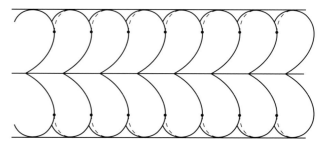

Fig. 5. Basic feather unit is drawn too high.

When starting the feather unit too far from the top guideline, the feathers look like fingers (fig. 6). To correct this, start a little closer to the guideline.

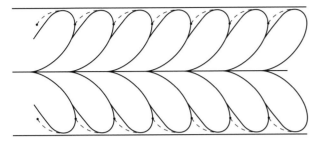

Fig. 6. Basic feather unit is drawn too low.

Rule #2

The top of the heart should be round and the size should be consistent for each feather. Learning to draw feathers in a consistent size (width) becomes easy with practice, without a template or tool. Feathers have a more natural look if there is slight variation from feather to feather.

When the top of the feather unit is drawn like an oval, it will look like this (fig. 7). To correct it, practice drawing an actual circle instead.

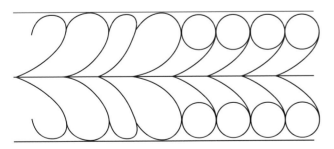

Fig. 7. Basic feather unit is not consistent width and not circular.

If you are still having trouble with this common mistake, try using a guide, such as a circle template or a coin for a few practice feathers (fig. 7). This should help to achieve a more consistent width. Over the years quilters have often used coins as a template when drawing feathers.

Rule #3

Continue drawing to the spine. Pay close attention to the spot where the feather unit touches the spine and the spot you started drawing it. Draw a line to connect these spots which should be perpendicular to the spine (fig. 8). For practice, actually drawing this line can be helpful, but eventually you will just imagine the line. This will keep feathers looking upright along the spine and not fall over. The spot where the basic feather unit meets the spine does not stop abruptly but flows into the spine and becomes the spine.

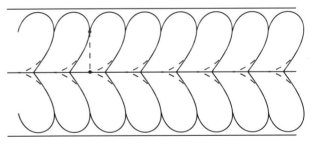

Fig. 8. Basic feather unit is not perpendicular to the spine.

The most common mistake when drawing feathers is that the feathers are not perpendicular to the spine. To correct this, swing in a little deeper as you come to the spine. Remember to make the pencil line flow into the spine.

Rule #4

The actual shape of a feather looks like a teardrop but what we draw instead is a half-heart shape. When half-heart shapes connect along the spine, they combine to make teardrop shapes. If a teardrop were drawn, there would be unneeded double lines of marking pencil on the fabric.

The spine is drawn first followed by the right side of a half-heart shape; then another right side of a half-heart is drawn, connecting it to the previous half-heart shape. Always think of the complete teardrop shape of the feather even though you are only drawing the half-heart shape of a feather unit. (Refer to figure 4, page 24)

Fig. 9. Draw feathers while looking at the feather pattern.

Freehand Feathers

Always keep in mind **the rules** when drawing feathers.

It is time to start drawing your own feathers —freehand. On a piece of paper; trace the spine and the top and bottom guidelines from my simple feather pattern. Move my pattern out from underneath your paper and place it in front of you to look at while drawing your own feathers (fig. 9). I still have a feather drawing to look at while I am drawing feathers on fabric. Now, carefully draw one simple feather. Repeat tracing the spine, the top, and bottom guidelines to complete three feathers.

Feather Drawing Alert #1

Students often ask: should the top and bottom feathers meet at the same place on the spine? My answer is it doesn't matter, some will and others won't. When drawing on a straight spine, if you start at the same place with the top and bottom feathers and the feather units are all the same width, they will meet at the same place on the spine. This can look odd, like hearts on a stick.

When drawing feathers on a curved line, there will be more feathers on the outside of the curve than on the inside of it. Because of this, the feathers cannot always meet at the same place on the spine. My recommendation is to not think about this when drawing feathers. Try to keep your feathers consistent in width and let them meet where they will at the spine. They will look normal and natural.

Feather Drawing Alert #2

Some students think of a heart shape drawn a little differently than I draw a heart. I call their version a stylized heart and this will not work for the basic feather unit (fig. 10). If this is how you visualize a heart, try thinking of something else for your feather unit. Try visualizing your ear, a comma or an apostrophe. Then try practicing with this in mind.

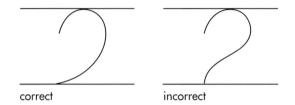

correct   incorrect

Fig. 10. Half-heart shape of basic feather unit

Drawing feathers takes practice, so be patient and things will improve the more you practice. Go slowly, draw carefully, and don't rush. The good news is most corrections will be minor and the more you draw feathers, the better they will become. Use another piece of paper and try drawing the simple practice feather freehand three more times.

The most common feathers have a curved spine. These are often called undulating feathers and look beautiful on the borders of quilts. Feathers are rarely drawn on the straight line that we started with but it is easier to explain basic feather drawing by using a straight spine. You will find drawing feathers on a curved line much easier and more forgiving.

Designing Feathers to Fit Borders

On many of my quilts I want the feathers to go around an outside border, to be symmetrical from side to side and top to bottom, and to turn the corner consistently. We will use an easy paper-folding technique to create a curved spine pattern. This pattern will be placed on the quilt top to mark the spine. Start with the exact dimensions of the quilt top. Draw a small diagram on paper to visualize this (fig. 11).

The finished size of the quilt top we will use is 60" x 60" and the borders are 6" wide. Always work with the measurements for the finished size of the border. This is where the feathers are drawn. Take the 6" corners out of the equation: subtract 12" from 60". The area we are making the spine pattern for is 48" x 6". Because that would need a large piece of paper, divide the length measurement in half and the paper-folding exercise will be done with a 24"x 6" piece of paper. Use a heavier paper called artist drawing paper. It is available on 18"x 24" pads.

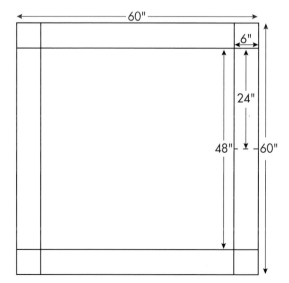

Fig. 11. Exact size of quilt

Because the paper is heavier than copy paper, it is easy to draw along the edge.

Fold this paper in half lengthwise. This will determine how many undulations there will be. Fold in half again for more undulations. The folded paper will be square now and it will measure 6" x 6" (figs. 12a–c). Be sure to keep the folds of this square on the right and left (raw edges will be top and bottom).

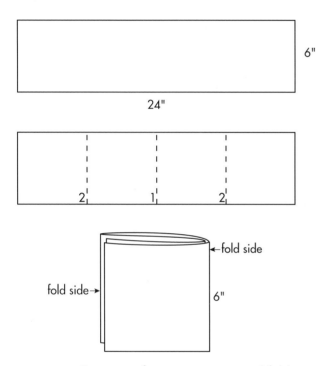

Figs. 12a–c. Cut paper for spine pattern and fold.

Marks will be made on this square to determine how deep or how flat the curve will be for the spine. To make a deeper curve use a mark that is less than 1½" and to make a gentler curve use a mark that is more than 1½". Using a 3" mark will result in a straight line. We will use the measurement of 1½" and make an average curve.

Make a mark 1½" down from the top right side. Make a mark 1½" up from bottom left side. Find the very center of this folded piece and make a mark. Draw a line to connect the marks. This will look like a gentle "S" curve (figs. 13a and b).

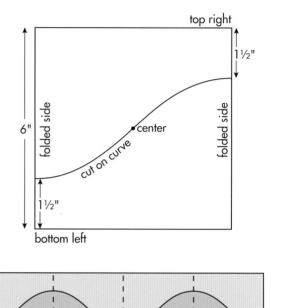

Figs. 13a and b. Mark paper to determine center spine. Cut on curved line.

Cut on the drawn line. There will be two patterns. Either one will work. The quilt is square and the pattern will work for all four sides. Use it to mark the spine directly on the quilt top. I like to place the non-curved edge of the pattern along the seam line (inside) of the border for accuracy. Figure 14, page 29, shows two different corners depending on which side of the paper is used.

To complete the corners, make a corner pattern as follows:

Cut a 6" square. Mark the same 1½" marks on the bottom right and the top left, as shown. Fold on the diagonal, sketch a curve, and then cut on the line (fig. 15a). Use this pattern to complete the corners (fig. 15b).

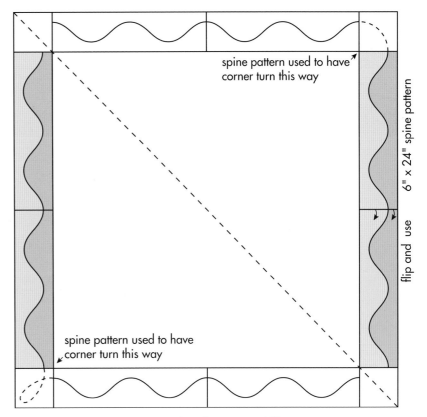

Fig. 14. Use spine pattern on borders. Two different ways to turn corners are shown.

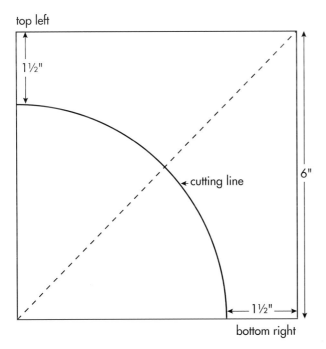

Fig. 15a.

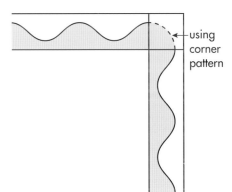

Fig. 15b. Corner pattern

Here are some different corner options (fig. 16).

Fig. 16. Corner feather options

This great technique can be done for any size quilt. Easily make your feather fit any size border. Dividing the border measurement by three will also work and this might be needed to get the amount of undulations needed. Wider borders can be made with a deep curve and the open area can be filled with feather tendrils or feather motifs (fig. 17).

Fig. 17. Deeper curves on the spine allow for space to use tendrils.

For a Rectangular Quilt

Most quilts that go on a bed are rectangular. When designing for a rectangular quilt make two spine patterns, one for the length and one for the width. Most often the width measurement is only slightly smaller than the length measurement. Make a diagram of the quilt and do the math a second time for the width versus the length. This quilt is 56" x 60" with 6" borders (fig. 18). The spine pattern for the 60" length is done as described earlier. For the 56" width, subtract the corners (12") and the area to make the spine pattern is 44" x 6". Divide 44" in half and cut the paper 22" x 6". Use the same undulations (folding the paper lengthwise) and the same measurements for marks (1½") used for the 60" length (fig. 19).

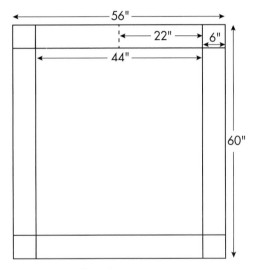

Fig. 18. Exact size of quilt

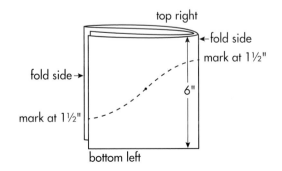

Fig. 19. Spine pattern for rectangular quilt. Make a pattern for the border width.

The width pattern will look slightly squished compared to the length. Visually it works because the undulations and the feathers height are the same. If it visually doesn't work, try folding one side into thirds and see if that works better. I have mostly used the first option and have had good success.

Drawing Feathers on Curved Spines

Practice drawing feathers on a curved spine using the curved spine pattern you made. Take a second piece of paper, cut 6" x 24". Lay the spine pattern on the paper matching the edges and draw the center spine line. Make guidelines on the top and bottom of this spine.

To easily draw consistent guidelines, use a compass. Set the compass at 1¼". This will make the guidelines smaller than the finished size of the border because the feathers should not be drawn to the edges of the border. Place the metal point of the compass on the spine. Drag it along the spine, marking with the compass pencil evenly 1¼" from both sides of the spine. This makes perfect 1¼" guidelines (fig. 20).

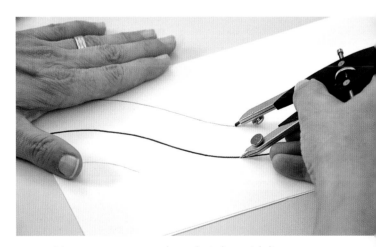

Fig. 20. Use a compass to draw height guidelines.

I do not mark these guidelines directly on the fabric, only on the paper. If desired, place the pattern under your border while freehand drawing the feathers on the fabric. Take a thick black marker and darken the spine line and the top and bottom guidelines. Lay this pattern under the border and easily see the guidelines while drawing on the fabric. If the fabric is dark or busy, use a light box.

Practice

It is now time to practice drawing feathers on a curved spine (fig. 21). Minor changes happen as you draw feathers along a curved spine. Remember to look at a feather drawing when drawing feathers. Draw four or five feathers on the top of the spine and then draw four or five feathers on the bottom of the spine.

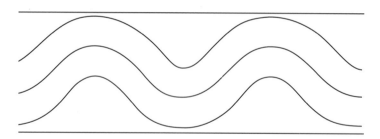

Fig.21. Diagram 17: Practice drawing feathers on a curved spine using top and bottom guidelines.

It is very important to remember **rule #3** (fig. 8, page 25). As you draw the feather unit, keep the feather upright as you move along the curved spine (fig. 22).

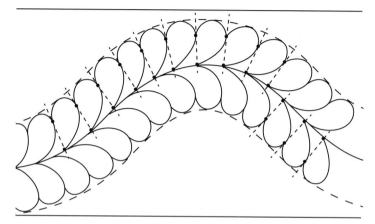

Fig.22. Drawing feathers on a curved spine. Rule #3—keep the basic feather unit perpendicular to the center spine.

Continue until you are done with this practice undulating feather. Look at your feather— it looks very pretty! Now it is time to look at it more carefully. Go through each of **the rules** and make sure each feather unit follows all of **the rules**. If not, make the minor changes to correct the mistakes. Your feather will look beautiful (fig. 23)!

Fig.23. Beautiful feathers drawn on a curved spine

Some Advice for Drawing Your Best Feathers

♦ I like to use my hand as a tool or guide when drawing feathers. I draw with my right hand. I place my left hand on the paper or fabric and for the top feathers, my thumb is placed near the spine and my hand (along the first finger) is at a right angle to the thumb (fig. 24). This isolates the spine so it looks more like a straight line and I can keep the feathers perpendicular to the spine more easily. For the bottom feathers, I place my hand in same configuration, except my thumb is near the bottom guideline. This also helps keep the fabric from shifting while marking the actual quilt.

Fig. 24. Using hand to help draw feathers

♦ Feathers on an inside curve look a little different than feathers on an outside curve. Inside curve areas take practice to get the feather to look right. There are less feathers on an inside curve than on an outside curve (fig. 25).

♦ Continue drawing practice feathers on the curved spine. Turn the long paper over and practice on the back side. Repeat this exercise two or three more times.

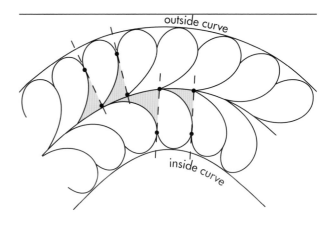

Fig. 25. Feathers on the inside curve look more elongated. Basic feather unit remains the same.

Drawing Motif Feathers

Now that you are drawing beautiful feathers on a curved spine, we will try some motif feathers. There are many shapes that can be used as a center spine. The shape we will try is a circle.

Feathered Wreath

Start with a circle as the spine and this will become a feathered wreath. Make a circle that measures 4" by setting the compass at 2". To make an inner guideline, move the compass to 1" and draw a smaller circle. To make an outer guideline, move the compass to 3" and make a larger circle (fig. 26).

Trace my "Feathered Wreath" (page 87) before drawing your own freehanded. Once you have traced my wreath, place it where you can see it and draw your own feathers on the circle you drew.

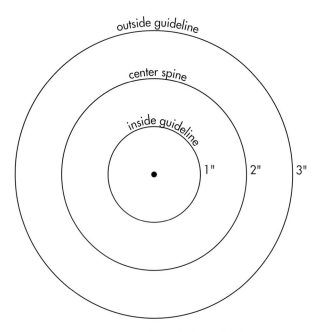

Fig. 26. Center spine and guidelines for feather wreath

Some Important Considerations for Drawing Feather Wreaths

◆ Keep the same orientation of the paper. Don't turn it as you are drawing the feathers. When drawing on a quilt it would be hard to turn the quilt, so don't be tempted to do this when practicing. You will be drawing feathers in all directions.

◆ Draw feathers clockwise, starting at the top. Draw all of the outside feathers first. As you are coming around from the bottom and going up the left side, stop when you are about four or five feathers from connecting the feathers at the top. Pretend you are drawing the remaining feathers. Lift your pencil from the paper and *air-draw* to give you an idea of how to accurately draw the feathers to connect perfectly (fig. 27). You don't want to end up with space for half of a feather. With practice this will be easy!

◆ Next draw the inside feathers. Look at the drawing of the feather to make sure you start the feather in the correct direction. Start

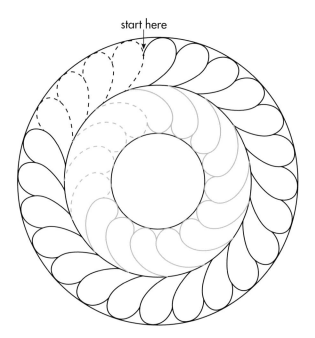

Fig. 27. Draw feathers clockwise. Air-draw when you are four or five feathers from connecting with the starting feathers. Next, draw the inside feathers.

at the top and draw clockwise on the inside of the spine line (fig. 27, page 34). Remember there will be fewer feathers on the inside and these feathers will look a little different—more elongated. The same method for connecting the ending feathers to the starting feather is used.

♦ When working on the actual quilt, make a template out of plastic or heavy paper. Use this template to draw the spine (circle) directly on the fabric, then draw the feathers on the fabric. I draw a practice feather on paper the exact size I will be using on the quilt. This is the drawing I look at when drawing the feathers on the quilt.

Designing Wholecloth Feathers

We are ready to move on to wholecloth feather designs. These designs look more complex, but when broken down into manageable steps, they are easy. Every feather starts with a spine and the feather unit is drawn on the spine, sometimes on both sides of the spine, or sometimes on one side. You can draw any feather creation imaginable with that basic concept!

These wholecloth feather designs can be made as small quilt projects as I have done or they can be used in open areas on bigger quilt projects. They can be drawn any size. My patterns can be enlarged or reduced to fit any quilt. The concept in this section is based on drawing ¼ of the design, or one quadrant, and then repeating it in the remaining three quadrants. It can start out looking very simple, but once you see the repeating feathers it becomes more complex and beautiful.

Plume Feather

The plume feather has been one of my favorite motifs for years. This simple feather uses the same concepts as designing wholecloth feathers. It has four quadrants and a simple plume shape that is repeated.

I use tracing paper on a roll to design wholecloth feathers. Refer to the supplies section (page 10) for details. When designing on tracing paper, place a piece of white paper underneath the tracing paper to have good visibility. We will use a 6½" square for this plume feather. I often draw this 6½" square on white paper and place this under the tracing paper.

Step 1

On a small piece of tracing paper, draw a 6½" square. Fold the paper in half lengthwise and widthwise, open the paper, and mark straight lines on these folds. This will designate the four quadrants. Also draw lines on the diagonal of each quadrant (fig. 28).

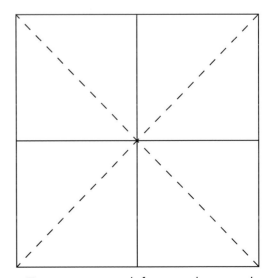

Fig. 28. Tracing paper with four quadrants and diagonals—Step 1

Step 2

For this particular design I started with a circle in the center of the four quadrants. Use a circle template to draw a perfect circle. Working in one quadrant, lightly sketch a center spine that looks like a plume on ⅛ of the paper (fig. 29).

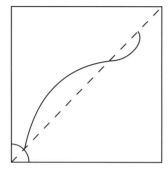

Fig. 29. Plume feather motif—Step 2

Step 3

Fold the tracing paper along the diagonal line and trace the opposite side of that quadrant. When the tracing paper is opened, the plume spine is now complete for that quadrant and looks symmetrical (fig. 30).

Fig. 30. Plume feather motif—Step 3

Step 4

On one side of the spine draw feathers, keeping in mind the basic feather unit (fig. 31).

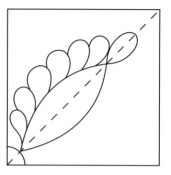

Fig. 31. Plume feather motif—Step 4

Step 5

Fold the quadrant on the diagonal and trace these feathers on the spine of the opposite side of the quadrant (fig. 32).

Fig. 32. Plume feather motif—Step 5

Step 6

Open the tracing paper and see how the feathers on this quadrant look.

If you are happy with the feathers, fold the tracing paper along the quadrant lines and trace the remaining three quadrants (fig. 33, page 37).

You now have a beautiful feather motif that was EASY to create!

If you were not happy with the feathers on the first quadrant—try again on a new piece of tracing paper.

Fig. 33. Plume feather motif—Step 6

Wholecloth Feather Designs

We are now ready to begin more complex designs. Look at Section Six: Feather Patterns and Projects to see the variety of beautiful feather designs that can be created using this concept. These designs are based on working in one quadrant, perfecting it, and repeating it three more times.

We will use a 6¾" square to design. This is the size used for the wholecloth feathers in the pattern section of this book and is ¼" of the completed design. When using the patterns directly from the book, the complete design will

be 13½". These would work nicely in a 15" area on a quilt or small 15" quilts can be made. Some of my finished quilts are 18" squares and the patterns from the book can be enlarged to fit a larger area.

Step 1 (Refer to step 1 of plume feather, page 35, this is done exactly the same in a bigger size.)

Draw a 13½" square on tracing paper. Fold the tracing paper in half and crease. Open it and fold in half the opposite direction and crease. Open the tracing paper and draw these lines to indicate four quadrants. Fold the tracing paper along the diagonal of the quadrants and draw these lines. Set this full-size tracing paper aside for now.

Step 2

With a black marking pen, draw a 6¾" square on white paper with a diagonal line. In the bottom right corner indicate the center of the complete design (fig. 34). Place this base quadrant under the tracing paper and use as a constant to draw the feathers.

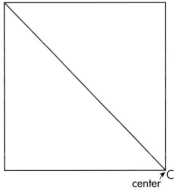

Fig. 34. Base quadrant for a wholecloth feather design. Make a 6¾" square with the center indicated in the bottom right corner.

Step 3

Prepare some 7"–8" squares of tracing paper. Lay one of these pieces of paper on top of the base quadrant prepared in Step 2. On one side of the square along the diagonal line, sketch an interesting line for a spine. This can take a few tries to find a spine that fits nicely and feathers can be drawn easily. Sometimes it is hard to create an interesting spine. Try your initial: it can be a great spine and an easy place to start. I will use my "S" initial for this segment of instruction (fig. 35a). My quilt PEACH PARFAIT (page 106) is the result of this exercise!

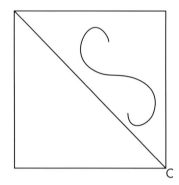

Fig. 35a. Center spine drawn in ⅛ area

Here are some important things to consider when drawing the center spine:

◆ When sketching spines, make sure to leave room to draw the feathers on each side of the spine to start, however it is fine to have feathers drawn on only one side.

◆ Think about the center area of the complete design when planning the center spine. How will that area look when all four quadrants are completed?

◆ Occasionally, I echo the feathers after quilting them and like to leave room for this.

◆ I use spirals often to end feathers and fill spaces; these can be incorporated when drawing spines or feathers.

Fig. 35b. Two feather designs use initials as the center spine. The first design uses an R and the second design uses a J. Try your initial—see what you come up with!

◆ Think about the filler to be stitched surrounding the feathers; it is nice to leave room for this.

◆ I often use a double spine and then fill the space between with small circles. I call these "Peas in a Pod" and used this on my quilt PEACH PARFAIT, page 106, featured in this segment.

Step 4

Once you have a spine you like, draw feathers on the spine. Next, fold your small piece of tracing paper along the diagonal line and trace the feathers on the other side. Open the tracing paper and see how this quadrant looks.

Fig. 36. Draw feathers on center spine on right ⅛ (black). Fold tracing paper on diagonal and trace left side. Add more elements: tendrils and curlicues (orange). Add circles in spine (pink).

Draw feathers on the center spine. Fold on the diagonal and trace on the opposite side – **black.**

Add more elements: tendrils and curlicues – orange.

Add circles to the spine area – **pink** (fig. 36).

Important Feather Drawing Alert

As you can see by looking at my patterns, when drawing feathers sometimes the height varies to fill an area. Now that you have experience drawing simple feathers, the height guideline rule can be broken!

If you like what you have created, move on to the next step; if not, try again with a different spine.

Step 5

Next, draw on the 13½" square prepared earlier. Place the design created on the smaller piece of tracing paper under the larger tracing paper and trace the first quadrant. Be careful to have the center of the design positioned in the center of the larger square. Trace all four center areas. This can be done by folding the tracing paper and tracing the opposite side.

Some reworking of the center area may be needed. Draw at least one repeat on the side. A motif or an additional feather may need to be added where the designs meet. You do not need to draw all four quadrants completely. You now have a beautiful wholecloth feather design (fig. 37, page 40)!

Fig. 37. Draw one quadrant on full-size tracing paper. Draw all centers. Draw one additional side to see how they meet (Step 5).

Fig. 38. Tracing paper design and marking on the fabric

opposite: Project Nine: PEACH PARFAIT, detail, full quilt on page 106

To use wholecloth designs for your quilt project, make the tracing-paper drawing visible by using a black marking pen to redraw over the pencil lines. Because these designs are a repeat, you only need to redraw one quadrant. Use this one quadrant to mark all four quadrants on the fabric. I often redraw the center area and the sides to have better accuracy when drawing on the fabric (fig. 38). Lay the tracing paper pattern on white paper for better visibility when marking the top.

I hope you have enjoyed learning to draw feathers. The more you practice the easier it will be for you to create your own beautiful and unique feather designs. Look at my nine wholecloth feather projects for ideas on spines, tendrils, and curlicues.

41

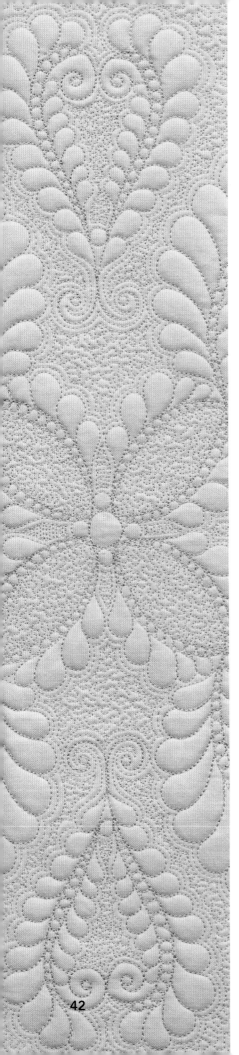

Machine Quilting Feathers

This section will start with the basics of free-motion quilting before attempting marked designs such as feathers. We will do practice exercises for a basic feather, cover more complex feather motifs next, and finish with wholecloth feather designs. After you have practiced, you will see that it is easier than you imagined to stitch beautiful feathers.

Basic Free-motion Information

I have loved free-motion quilting for over 25 years. It took practice to become comfortable and relaxed. Free-motion quilting is done using a darning foot on your machine and lowering the feed dogs. This allows you to move the quilt freely in any direction to stitch designs with curves such as feathers.

Many of you have attempted free-motion quilting and know it feels unusual at first, but the more you practice, the easier and more comfortable it feels. If you have never attempted to free-motion quilt, practice the basics before starting on feathers. I recommend everyone do the next practice exercise, even if you have free-motion experience. It is a good way to warm up and also try my method for these concepts.

Basic Skills of Free-motion Quilting

Let's get started! The following are the rules I follow to be successful. The first concept is once the feed dogs are lowered, you will be moving the quilt to create the stitches. For regular sewing, the feed dogs move the fabric to create stitching and the stitch length is set to a specific number. Once the feed dogs are gone, the quilt will stay in place unless you move the quilt to create the stitches. Your fingers are the feed dogs in free-motion quilting!

Please note: I refer to the darning foot I use as the traditional darning foot in the basics skills section to differentiate from the BSR (BERNINA Stitch Regulator). The BSR is the one type of darning foot that does allow you to set a stitch length. The free-motion quilting methods described in this book are achieved using a traditional darning foot. This is the most common approach for free-motion quilting and I believe it teaches these techniques to the majority of the quilters.

If you have a BSR, refer to your dealer for specific directions for this foot. You can successfully do all the free-motion techniques taught in this book with either type of darning foot (fig. 1).

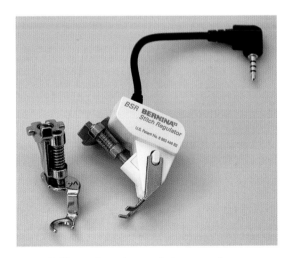

Fig. 1. BSR and traditional darning foot

Basic Skill # 1:
Securing starts and stops

When starting or ending a line of stitching, the stitches need to be secured by making 8 to12 very small stitches. These small stitches are made within about a ¼" area (fig. 2). The slower you move the quilt under the darning foot the smaller the stitches, and the faster you move the quilt under the darning foot, the bigger the stitches. When starting and stopping, move the quilt slowly to create these small stitches. Try to place these small stitches in inconspicuous places.

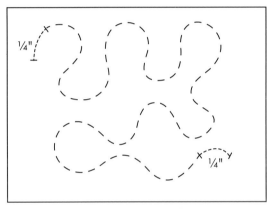

Fig. 2. Secure starts and stops with small stitches.

Basic Skill # 2:
Consistent stitch length

When free-motion quilting, other than the starts and stops, an average stitch length is desired. It takes practice to achieve this. The movement of the quilt under the darning foot is one factor that goes into creating stitch length. Moving the quilt at an even rate will help create a consistent stitch length. Another factor that goes into creating stitch length is sewing speed. This is how fast the needle is moving up and down. The sewing speed is controlled by your foot on the foot pedal.

These two factors need to work together to create a consistent stitch length throughout your quilt. Become comfortable moving the quilt easily and match the sewing speed to the movement of the quilt. If your stitches are too small, slow your sewing speed. If your stitches are too big, sew faster. This concept is stitch regulation. With practice you can become your own stitch regulator. I sew with my shoe off because I have better control of sewing speed on my foot pedal.

When free-motion quilting feather designs (a marked design), move the quilt slower to stay in control and on the marked line. Adjust the sewing speed to sew slower, matching the movement of the quilt. When free-motion quilting a no-mark design, like stipple quilting, you will move the quilt faster, adjusting sewing speed to sew faster to match the movement of the quilt.

Fig. 3. Nicely stitched feather and stippling: Project One: Vanilla Cream (detail of corner with small spiral feather wreath)

I never sew at the highest speed or the slowest speed on my machine. The sewing speed should be between medium and medium high and this will depend on how fast or slow you are moving the quilt under the darning foot. You can use the speed control on your sewing machine, if you have this option. Set it at medium for feathers and marked designs and set it at medium high for no-mark designs like stipple quilting. This feature is offered on most machines and is helpful for free-motion quilting.

Another way to think of the concept of achieving consistent stitch length in free-motion quilting is this: If your stitches are smaller than an average stitch, you are sewing too fast for the movement of the quilt— sew slower. If your stitches are bigger than an average stitch length, you are sewing too slow for the movement of the quilt—sew faster.

The average stitch length on most sewing machines is 2.5. This comes out to about 8 to 10 stitches per inch. I like my stitches a little smaller than this. When using a regular stitch (with feed dogs engaged), I use 2.0 for my stitch length. This comes out to about 12 to 14 stitches per inch. I feel that smoother curves are achieved with a slightly smaller than average stitch length.

I try to keep a consistent stitch length throughout my project. The only time I might alter this is when doing a small mini-stipple as filler in smaller areas (fig. 3). In this case, the stitches will need to be a little smaller to fill the area proportionally and have smooth stitches.

Basic Skill # 3:
Smooth and steady stitching

Placement of your fingers on the quilt is very important. I place my fingers on either side of the darning foot—at 9 and 3 o' clock and the needle is the center of the clock. My fingertips are about 1" to 2" from the needle (fig. 4).

Fig. 4. My hands and finger position at darning foot

Always keep your fingertips on the quilt while sewing. When you need to reposition your hands, stop sewing with the needle down, reposition fingertips, and start sewing again. If you move your hands off of the quilt while you are sewing, the quilt doesn't know what to do.

On a small piece, the quilt will not move (stay in place) and you will sew in place. This will create a knot or build-up of visible stitches and is not pretty. On a large project the quilt is usually touching you over your shoulder or on your chest. Once your fingertips come off of the quilt while still sewing, the quilt will move slightly as you move your body slightly, causing jerky and uneven stitches.

This concept took practice, but now it is ingrained in what I do. The instant I feel the need to move my hands, I stop sewing, the needle goes down and I move my fingertips to a better position that gives me more control for smooth and steady stitching.

Some students have said that once they reposition their fingertips and they start sewing again, an awkward stitch is made—either too big or not in the correct place. My method for starting smoothly is to take your first stitch when you start sewing again in the same spot or hole you stopped in. Slowly build up the speed of moving the quilt and your sewing speed.

Another way to explain this concept is you don't do two things at one time. Start sewing, then move the quilt. If you start sewing and move the quilt at the same time, an awkward or jerky stitch is made. Even though this is hard to explain, it is very important and is often the skill that students say is the most important thing they have learned to be successful at free-motion quilting.

Basic Skill #4:
Stitching order

It is easier working from the top of a quilt to the bottom. With free-motion quilting, you have the ability to go backward, meaning you can move the quilt toward your body. You are not directionally challenged as in regular sewing with the feed dogs engaged.

Although the quilt can be moved in any direction to sew with free-motion quilting, it is easier to see where to stitch if the quilt is moved away from you (working from top of quilt to bottom, figure 5). When stitching backwards or moving the quilt toward you, the stitches are made behind the darning foot, making it difficult to see. This is especially true for marked designs like feathers. I sew backwards when necessary, but prefer to work from top to bottom if possible.

Fig. 5. Work from top of quilt to bottom for good visibility.

When free-motion machine quilting, keep in mind these four basic skills. They are the foundation for successful free-motion machine quilting.

1st Practice Sample

It is time to start on our practice piece. This will be a good way to warm up and use these four basic skills.

Prepare a small practice quilt piece. I use muslin for practice. It is inexpensive and I can see my stitching easily. Don't use prints or white on white type of fabric. I use the same type of batting I will use for my quilt project. For this first practice piece, prepare a 12" square package of two pieces of muslin and one square of batting. Mark a straight line through the center of the muslin square in both directions to make four quadrants. Baste the three layers together with safety pins (fig.6).

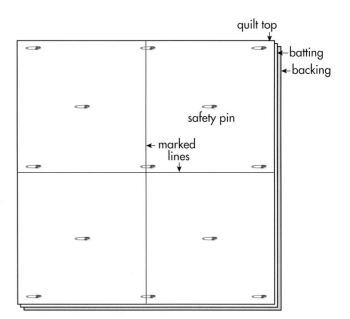

Fig. 6. 1st practice sample—mark and safety pin baste

Thread your machine top and bobbin with an average-weight cotton thread in a color to match your practice fabric. Use an appropriate needle for the thread selected. Place the darning foot on the sewing machine and lower the feed dogs. Place the straight-stitch throat on the machine, if available. Use the needle-down option when stopping to reposition your hands. The needle stops down in the quilt and the quilt will stay in place. I use rubber glove fingers on the first two fingers of each hand to allow me to have a light touch on the quilt. (Review the supplies mentioned in the Supplies Section, pages 10–21.)

When working on a practice piece, I treat it like a real quilt. Start in the center at the top. The first quadrant to quilt is the top right. The next quadrant will be the bottom right. The bulk of the quilt will always be left of your machine and the lesser amount is in the arm area of your machine. Turn the practice piece 180 degrees and repeat this for the third and fourth quadrants. This will work for any size project and will be explained again in Section Five: Quilting the Quilt – Start to Finish, pages 75–82.

In the first quadrant, sew some wavy lines in rows across the surface. Begin and end with the 8 to12 small stitches described in Basic Skill #1 (page 43). Start at the top of the quadrant. Lower the darning foot. Holding the top thread, take one stitch, moving the needle down and up. Lift the darning foot and bring the bobbin thread to the top of the quilt (fig. 7). Both threads should be under the darning foot.

Fig. 7. Bringing bobbin thread to the top of quilt

Position the darning foot so the needle starts in the same hole as the bobbin thread. Lower the darning foot and hold both threads with a little tension. Begin moving the quilt slowly to make the 8 to 12 small stitches.

Continue stitching, moving the quilt faster to make normal length stitches. Remove safety pins when you are about 1" to 2" away from them. When you are far enough away from the start, stop sewing with the needle down and clip threads at the surface. Carefully start sewing again. Make a continuous wavy line working from left to right, right to left, and down to fill the first quadrant (fig. 8). Keep in mind the concepts discussed in the Basic Skills.

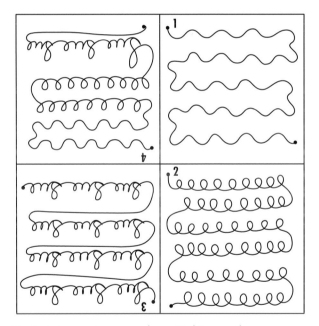

Fig. 8. 1st practice sample—stitching order

In the second quadrant, try sewing some simple loops. Secure both the starting and stopping stitches, even though this is a practice sample. It is important that these steps become ingrained.

In the next quadrant (following the proper stitching order), try writing your name in cursive. Your stitches should be more even and consistent as you have become more familiar with moving the quilt. If they aren't, think about the Basic Skills and apply them again. In the last quadrant, repeat the wavy lines, loops, and writing.

One last thing to check on this sample is stitch quality. Look at the front and back of the sample to see that the tensions are properly adjusted. Stitch quality for machine quilting can also be improved by using a straight-stitch throat plate.

If you have followed this advice and still have trouble, consider some of the recommendations given in the Supplies section. Use good quality thread, as well as a new and appropriate needle, and have your machine cleaned and oiled.

You have now completed your small practice piece. Feel free to repeat this practice exercise a few more times. The Basic Skills will be your foundation for success in free-motion quilting for both no-mark and marked designs.

Mind Your P's to Be Successful in Free-motion Quilting

Practice

It takes practice to become a successful free-motion quilter. I compare it to learning cursive handwriting. When we first learned cursive handwriting our teacher had us do page after page of repetitive work. The more we did this, the easier and better we became at handwriting. I call this a learned skill and anyone can learn if they take the time to practice.

Free-motion quilting is a learned skill and with practice anyone can be successful! Try practicing 15 minutes a day and with this repetitive work, you will quickly see improvement.

Patience

Be patient with yourself! It takes practice to achieve success with free-motion quilting. I have never had a new quilter come to class and do perfect stitching the first time. It is not going to happen. Set realistic expectations. Your first stitching won't look like your teacher's stitching who has been machine quilting for over 20 years. However, it won't take 20 years to be good at it. I was doing good work within the first six months I was machine quilting.

Be patient with your sewing machine. Sewing machines act up; thread breaks, tensions are off and your patience can wear thin. Stop and rethread both the top and the bobbin thread—95% of the time this solves the problem! If that does not solve the problem, more troubleshooting will be needed, but with patience you will figure it out!

Perseverance

Be stubborn! The student who comes to my machine quilting class and says: Teach me everything you know, I am determined to be a good quilter! That student will become a good machine quilter. Attitude is everything.

I truly believe I am a successful quilter because I am very stubborn. I practiced and figured it out! I have had students say to me that I must have had a knack for free-motion quilting. No, I had the same learning curve as anyone else. The reason I am successful is I worked hard and I persevered!!

Next, we will explore free-motion quilting the feather design.

Stitching Basic Feathers

The feather designs used in this book are marked designs. This means that you will use a fabric-marking pencil to mark the quilt top with the feather designs before layering and basting the quilt for machine quilting.

The perception is that a marked design is harder to do than a no-mark design. With practice a marked design can be done successfully. I stitch the feathers first on my quilt project and then fill with stipple quilting or variations around the feather. You may decide to do some no-mark fillers from the next section first if that is a more comfortable progression for you.

The methods for marking your quilt top are covered thoroughly in Section 5, pages 75–82. Some quilters do not enjoy these designs because of the time they take to mark. Hopefully, with good instruction and tools that make it easier, this step will be more enjoyable. Because I love feathers, I am willing to take the time to mark them to achieve the desired result. Following lines that have been marked on the top takes control when free-motion quilting. With practice, it becomes easier to follow the lines.

Here are some helpful suggestions:

♦ Think of the marked lines as guidelines. Try to stay as close to the guidelines as possible, but if you stray, gradually and smoothly come closer to the line again. A quick jerk back to the line is very noticeable. As long as you stay true to the design, it will look like the design once the marks are gone. I stay close to my lines because of many hours of practice, but I am not always perfectly on the line.

♦ Start at the top of the design and work down. This way you can always see the line that you need to follow. Sometimes, you may want to sew backwards to save time. This can be hard to do because the darning foot gets in the way visually. I rarely sew directly backwards because my stitches are never as smooth and consistent.

♦ The stitching order of the basic feather will be done in three paths—the center spine first, the left feathers, and then the right feathers, starting at the top of each path and ending at the bottom. This way you don't have to go directly backwards.

In the drawing feathers section, I recommended drawing feathers horizontally. When sewing feathers it is easier to stitch them vertically. There may be times on motif feathers and wholecloth feathers when you can do a more continuous path. These designs are more curved and don't have straight backward lines.

A frequently asked question is where should you look when free-motion quilting. A good comparison is to driving a car. When driving, your hands are on the steering wheel, but you are watching the road ahead of you. The steering wheel is visible, but you need to have the sight of the road ahead. In free-motion quilting you need to see where you are going, but also be aware of the needle. When analyzing this, I don't look ahead, or beyond the darning foot. I look just on the inside of the darning foot ahead of the needle (fig. 9). You can still see the marked line and this can be the perfect place for your eye to look.

I would rather free-motion quilt a feather than any other design. Feathers are forgiving and look nice even if they aren't exactly perfect. Not sewing on the lines perfectly every time adds to the beauty of this natural, organic design. A nice rhythm is developed when sewing a feather.

The type of feather I use the most is the one I refer to as a traditional feather. This is the feather we covered mainly in the drawing feathers section.

2nd Practice Sample

For this practice piece, prepare two 12" square pieces of muslin and a 12" square of batting. Mark one 12" square of muslin with the simple feather design from the pattern 3 Simple Feathers on page 85.

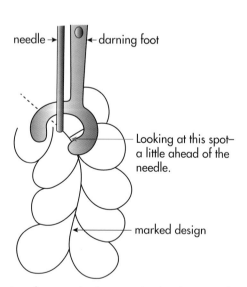

Fig. 9. Darning foot and where to look when stitching a marked design

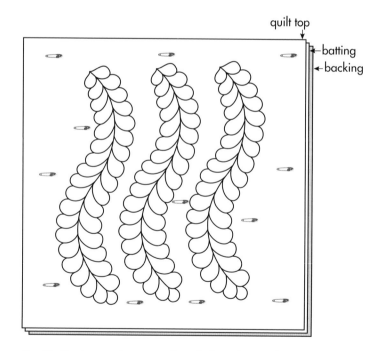

Fig. 10. 2nd practice sample—3 Simple Feathers

Lay the muslin square on top of the designs and trace with a silver marking pencil. Baste the three layers together with safety pins. Thread your machine top and bobbin with an average-weight cotton thread in a color to match your practice fabric.

To free-motion quilt the feather design, remember how the feather is made. It has a center spine with feathers on both sides of the spine. It will take three paths to sew (fig. 11). In relationship to the top of the quilt, start quilting at the top of the feather.

stitching order in figure 11. Sew the teardrop shape of the feather to the spine and re-stitch or backtrack to get to the next feather (figs. 12 and 13).

Fig. 12. Re-stitching feather

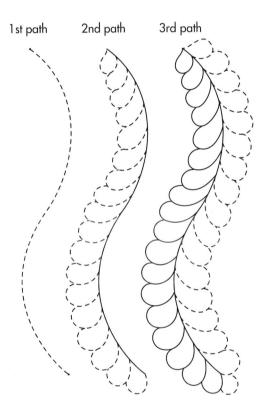

1st path   2nd path   3rd path

Fig. 11. Feather stitching order

Fig. 13. Detail of re-stitched area

Sew the spine first. If the feather is on the border of a quilt, sew the spine down the entire border. Come back to the top of the feather and sew down the left side of the feather. Follow the

Continue in this manner until this side of the feather is complete. Go back to the top and sew the right side of the feather to complete the design. Re-stitching makes the feather a continuous-line design. It is crucial to re-stitch as close as possible to the first stitches—ideally exactly the same, hole for hole, which is hard to do. Traditional feathers are much easier than you might think. A rhythm is developed with the repetitive, back-and-forth motion of sewing.

If you have trouble re-stitching perfectly, try leaving a small space between the feathers. The feather is drawn on the fabric the same as before. Use one of the simple feathers from the previous practice sample. Stitch using the same three paths as described for the traditional feather. This can look very pretty and may be a little easier for some. I still think of this as a traditional feather.

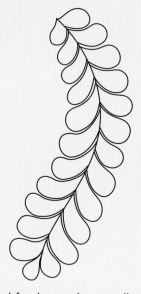

Traditional feather with a small space and no re-stitching

Repeat the exercise with the remaining two simple feathers on the practice piece. After stitching the three simple feathers, compare the first one you stitched with the third and you will see improvement!

Two common things happen when free-motion quilting marked designs such as feathers:

♦ **The first thing** you may notice is your stitches are very small. This happens because you are moving the quilt slowly to stay on the line and you are sewing too fast. Slow your sewing speed.

♦ **The second thing** that happens is quilters turn the quilt from side to side to follow the marked curved line. Don't do this. This will make it harder to achieve smooth and consistent stitching. Keep the quilt straight on and do all movements, side to side and up and down.

Direction of Stitching Feathers

I recommend you sew from the top of the feather down, in relationship to how it is drawn on the quilt. The feather can be drawn with the round part of the teardrop down or up. The main consideration is how the design is positioned on the quilt. Always work from the top of the quilt, whichever way the feather is drawn on that border (fig. 14).

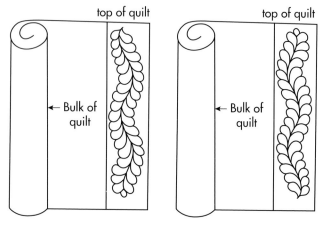

Fig. 14. Stitch from top of quilts, feathers drawn two ways

Stitching Feather Motifs

Now we will look at motif feathers, such as feathered wreaths and feathered plumes. The stitching order will be slightly different for each design. This is a good intermediate step, before we move on to the more complex wholecloth feathers.

3rd and 4th Practice Samples

Prepare two more practice quilt samples using two 12" squares muslin and one 12" square batting for each one. Mark one square with the feathered wreath design and one with the feathered plume design. (See pages 87 and 89 in Section Six: Feather Patterns and Projects). Baste the sample with safety pins.

Feathered Wreath Motif

Starting at the top of the sample, stitch the spine first, following the circle clockwise. Keep the quilt package straight—don't turn. This will be awkward at first. You will be going backwards as you come up and around the left side. There will be a small segment where you may have a blind spot. I tilt the quilt package slightly, to see the line. Continue to the outside feathers and work clockwise. When you arrive at the top, continue to the inside feathers and stitch clockwise to complete the feathered wreath in a continuous stitching line (fig. 15).

For a large feathered wreath, divide it in half and stitch the right side with three paths starting each path at the top. Turn it 180 degrees and stitch the opposite side with three paths, starting each path at the top. You will not need to stitch backwards for long distances on the left side using this approach. See photo, page 54.

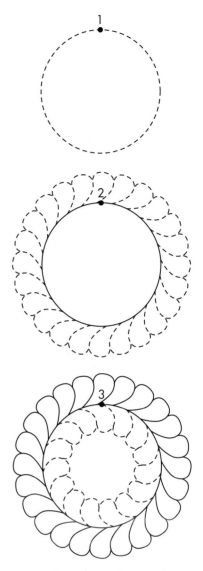

Fig. 15. Wreath stitching order

FABULOUS Feathers & Fillers DESIGN & MACHINE-QUILTING TECHNIQUES ◆ Sue Nickels

Feathered Plume Motif

This motif feather will be stitched like the wreath. Work clockwise and start with the top right plume. Stitch the spine, including the loop. Next, stitch the feathers clockwise on the outside of the center spine. At the top, re-stitch to get to the feathers on the other side. At the end of this plume, use the center circle to get to the next plume (bottom right) and repeat the steps in the first plume. Next, stitch the bottom left plume and then finish with the top left plume (fig. 16). See photo, page 56.

I sometimes use fillers like stipple quilting in the inner area of the plume. We will cover this in Section Four and you can come back and try this on your sample (fig. 17).

Fig. 16. Plume stitching order—stitch the top right plume first and work clockwise to complete the remaining three plumes.

Fig. 17. Inner area of plume with stipple quilting.

opposite: Feathered wreath motif sample

Stitching Wholecloth Feathers

The next practice sample will be a whole-cloth feather design. These designs are more complex and take some thought to determine the order of stitching.

5th Practice Sample

Prepare two 12" square pieces of muslin and a 12" square of batting. Mark one 12" square of muslin with the wholecloth design PEACH PARFAIT (page 107). Lay the muslin square on top of the design and trace with a silver marking pencil. I like thinner threads for wholecloth feathers. These include 50/2 cotton, 60/2 cotton, and 100-weight silk. Use the appropriate needle for the thread selected.

Let's break down one quadrant of a wholecloth feather. The quadrant can be divided in half (⅛ of design). Find the most continuous spine. Stitch the spine. Continue without stopping to stitch one side of the feathers. Then follow back on the opposite side feathers. All of this stitching can be done in one continuous path.

This smaller project can be stitched in many different directions and the piece can be turned at the machine to see the lines better. When I reach a spot where I either can't see the line easily or I can't go any farther, I stop, secure the stitches, and clip the threads.

This design has little curlicues. Don't end at a curlicue, instead re-stitch and continue on. Don't re-stitch more than 1" or 2" in any one place. It is better to stop and start again (fig. 18).

When this eighth is stitched, repeat with the other side. When a design has a center motif, this is done last. Because the center is a main focus, good stitching is needed and you will be warmed up and feeling confident in your skills.

Fig. 18. Stitching order for wholecloth feather PEACH PARFAIT, page 107
　　1–Center spine
　　2–Feathers

The stitching for PEACH PARFAIT was done in a continuous format and in this order: stitch the spines, feathers, and then the curlicues.

opposite: Feathered plume motif sample

The small circles are done after the feathers and in a continuous format. Stitch half circles on one side and then stitch the half circles on the other side (fig. 19). I like to call these "peas in a pod."

Fig. 19. Pea in a pod:
    3–One side of circles between spine
    4–Second side of circles

PROJECT NINE: PEACH PARFAIT, *detail, full quilt on* page 106

The small feathers are stitched next on PEACH PARFAIT.

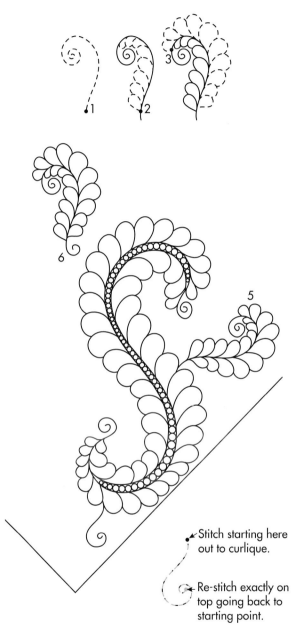

Stitch starting here out to curlique.

Re-stitch exactly on top going back to starting point.

Fig. 20. 5–Stitch small feather on side.
6–Stitch small feather center top.

I often echo my feathers. Echo quilting is done after all the feather stitching is complete. The last stitching to do is the filler and I often use stipple quilting. This will surround the feathers (see detail of PROJECT NINE: PEACH PARFAIT on pages 58–59). Echo quilting and stipple quilting will be covered in Section Four: Machine Quilting Fillers. Come back later to echo and stipple this practice sample.

Quilting Wholecloth Projects

The small projects in this book are made of four quadrants. I recommend doing a practice sample using one quadrant of the design selected. This will help you determine the easiest path to follow for that particular design. There is most likely more than one approach for each design that will work.

Once you have practiced, start on the actual project. Begin with the top right quadrant (fig. 21). Stitch this quadrant in the order determined on the practice sample. Next stitch the bottom right quadrant. Turn the quilt 180 degrees and repeat the third and fourth quadrants to finish the feathers. These small projects can be turned at the sewing machine to have better visibility following the lines. Next, echo the feathers if desired. Finish with fillers.

You have now completed five practice samples to learn the free-motion quilting techniques for sewing feathers. You should be feeling comfortable with the techniques we have covered so far. Feel free to repeat these exercises. Review the information in my basic skills and read my three P's for successful free-motion quilting often. We will now move on to fillers that will enhance the beautiful feathers you have stitched!

Fig. 21. Stitching order of wholecloth project

SECTION FOUR:
Machine Quilting Fillers

◇◇

I have always been inspired by antique quilts for quilting ideas. Many of the early quilters used hand stippling to fill in areas surrounding motifs like feathers to create dimension in their quilt. Small curved designs stitched very close together flatten the area next to a feather causing a dimensional look. In free-motion quilting, it is very easy to create these small jigsaw puzzle-piece shapes. This type of quilting is often referred to as fillers. We can use many different shapes to create these fillers that surround feathers, other quilting motifs, and appliqué (fig. 1).

We are going to cover many different ideas for fillers to surround and to fill within our wholecloth feathers. We will start with traditional stipple quilting and then explore other shapes that can add variety as fillers. These will include: loops, spirals, shells, echoing, and a new concept I call structured stippling. I refer to these ideas as no-mark designs because the quilt top is not marked. You will find it easier in the long run to create these shapes freehand.

My suggestion is to do some drawing of the shapes on paper first. Place a piece of paper or tracing paper on top of my design and trace over it. Next try drawing the design yourself on a blank piece of paper. See if this helps with each of the fillers we will cover.

We will also cover crosshatching as a filler. This is the one filler we will mark the background before basting the quilt.

Fig. 1. Beautiful stippling—PROJECT TWO, MINT JULEP, detail, full quilt on page 92

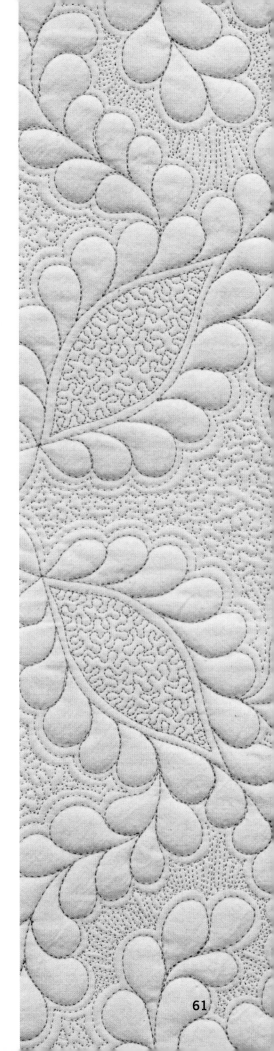

Traditional Stipple Quilting

This is the most common filler. It is easy to do and it looks great! The shape made when doing traditional stipple quilting looks like a little jigsaw puzzle piece (fig. 2).

Fig. 2. Traditional stipple quilting shapes

Here are some important guidelines to follow:

♦ Fill the space evenly. If there are open areas, this will create a bumpy, uneven look. The area that is filled should be even and flat.

♦ Keep the shapes a similar size. If the shapes are big and little, this also gives a bumpy and uneven look.

♦ Blend the shapes. Don't make them look like rows. They should mingle and mix. I stitch in a row format but it doesn't look like rows.

♦ Try not to cross over your stitching lines. It will look flatter and smoother if you don't cross over the stitching lines. Crossing

over your lines may happen occasionally, due to visibility issues; just keep it to a minimum.

The scale of the traditional stipple quilting is important. The shapes should be smaller than the feather they are surrounding. When the size of the stipple shapes are the same as the feather, the feather and stippling will all look the same and the feather disappears.

My diagrams show different sizes of stipple quilting (fig. 3, page 63). Some might think what I call large looks small, but if you think of it next to the feather it makes more sense. The size of stipple quilting on most of my small wholecloth projects is average, according to my diagram. The small traditional stipple quilting is often referred to as micro-stippling. I would use this only to fill in small areas, perhaps within a feather motif, not on the outside of a feather.

When stitching small stipple quilting, try practicing in smaller areas. We tend to fill an area proportionally and it is hard to go small in large areas. The stitch length also will need to be a little smaller to navigate the smaller curves and you will need to move the quilt slower, so sew slower. Remember, smaller stitches = smoother curves.

The thread you choose for your filler is crucial. I like to think of the filler as background stitching. It is not a main player, but a supporting member of the team. For this reason I tend to use finer threads. One of my favorite threads for stippling is a 50/2 cotton thread. It is slightly thinner than an average-weight thread and works perfectly in a supporting role. I also use

Large stippling

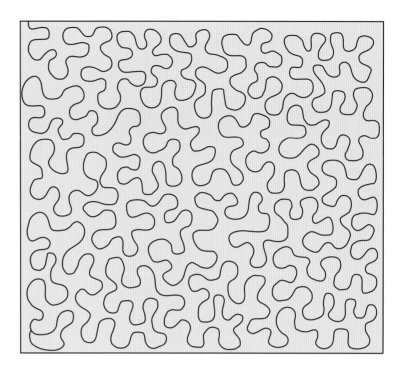

Average stippling

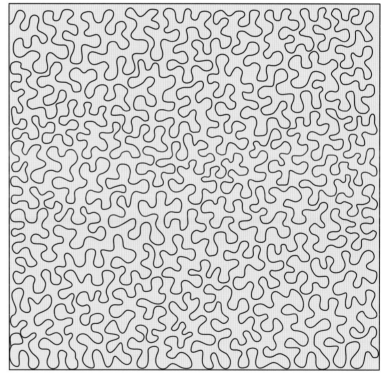

Small stippling

Fig. 3. Large, average, and small stipple quilting

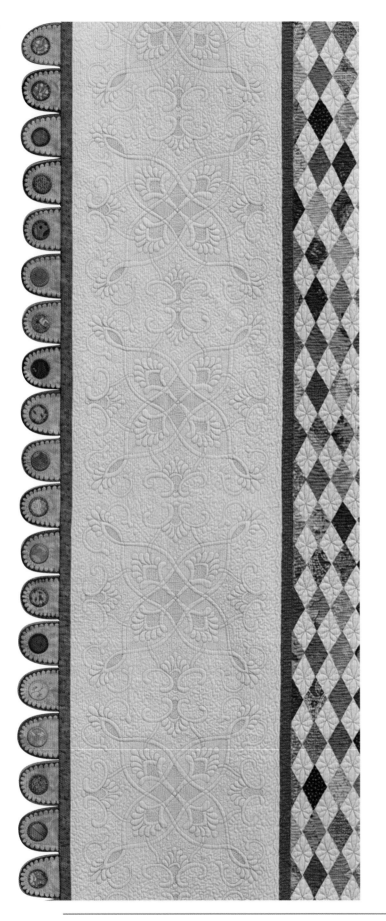

Detail of TEA AT TENBY. Full quilt on page 6.

60/2 cotton thread and 100-weight silk thread if the area is stitched heavily. A thicker thread can build up thread and look bulky.

The color of the thread is important also. I usually match the color of the thread to the fabric. This will also make it look more like a background. Sometimes selecting a slightly different color to stitch some areas with filler can give a very pretty shaded effect. TEA AT TENBY uses this approach in the border quilting (fig. 4).

1st Filler Practice Sample

For this practice piece, prepare a 12" square package of two pieces of muslin and one 12" square of batting. Mark a straight line through the center of the muslin square in both directions to make four quadrants. Baste the three layers together with safety pins. Review the Basic Skills in Section Three before starting.

The first quadrant will be for warm-up. In the top right quadrant, begin stitching at the top left corner and work to the right with a wavy line. Work back from the right to left. Continue these wavy lines for a few rows. Next, start making the waves deeper and more exaggerated, this is the shape that creates one piece of the puzzle. Continue to fill the whole top right quadrant.

You should be warmed up and ready to start some traditional stipple quilting in the lower right quadrant. Remember to draw some first on paper. Starting in the top left corner of the bottom right quadrant, work to the right making the little puzzle shapes (we are working in the large size; refer to the original diagram on page 63). Create the puzzle shapes so they are uneven.

When you are as far right as you can go (leave 1" margin around the whole practice sample to have something to hold onto with your right hand), drop down a little and start working back to left. Fill into the top row of shapes. Because you made the first row uneven, they will mingle and blend nicely. When you are back to the left side of this quadrant, drop down a little and work back to the right. Continue back and forth and down to complete this quadrant.

Look at what you have just done and review the guidelines listed above. How did you do? With practice you will get better and feel more relaxed. Eventually it will become natural and intuitive to stitch the stipple shapes.

Turn your practice sample 180 degrees and the third quadrant to stitch will be on the top right again. Starting at the top left corner, stitch the traditional stipple average size. Use the same order as the second quadrant. You will be making the shapes smaller and the area will be more densely quilted and lie flatter than the last quadrant (fig. 5). Look at what you have just stitched, reviewing the guidelines. I am sure you are getting better and more relaxed.

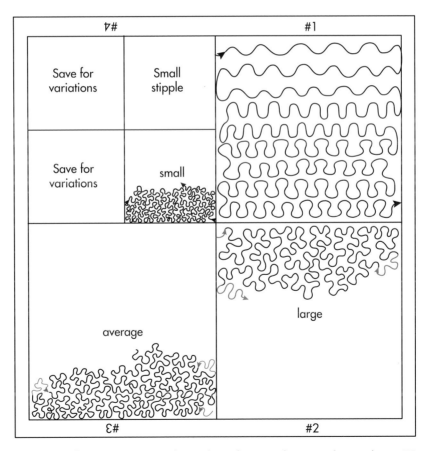

Fig. 5. Stipple practice sample and stitching order—stitch quadrant #1 and #2, turn 180 degrees, and stitch #3 and #4

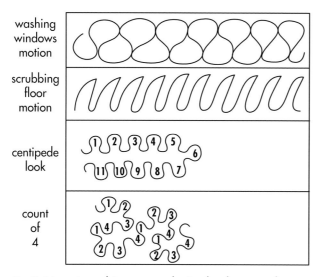

washing windows motion

scrubbing floor motion

centipede look

count of 4

Fig. 6. How to achieve round stipple shapes—keep stipple shape in clusters (count of four)

Fig. 7. Sample stitched

Some Common Questions

♦ *Why do I get pointed areas instead of smooth curves?*

There can be a few reasons for this. Stippling is like washing windows; the movement is very round and circular. Students sometimes are scrubbing the floor instead. This is more a back-and-forth movement that can create the points instead of curves. Also, moving the quilt slower and sewing slower can help (fig. 6).

♦ *Why can't I get the shapes to mingle nicely?*

It is important to think of the puzzle shape like a small cluster. I often think my shape looks like a gingerbread man cookie. There is a head, arms and legs. If you make many legs and arms it creates what I call the centipede look. It is hard to mingle the long awkward shapes. Sometimes I count the little arms and legs—one, two, three, four, and turn into another cluster of shapes (fig. 6).

For the last quadrant, divide this with your marking pencil into fourths. This will make smaller areas to work with the traditional stipple small. I work in the same exact order of stitching, the shape is just smaller. Your stitches will also need to be smaller, just not too tiny! You want to see an actual stitch made. Try this in two of the smaller squares. Save two of the smaller areas for other stipple variations you might want to see small (fig. 7, page 66).

When using traditional stipple quilting to surround your feathers, make sure to touch the feather frequently to accent the feather and make it pop out. You may want to echo your feather, and if you do, you will want the stipple to come right up to and touch the outermost echo. Use one of your practice sample feathers from Section Three and try some traditional stipple quilting surrounding it (fig. 8).

Fig. 8. Stipple should touch the feather or echo to create filler dimension.

Fig. 9. Sample stitched

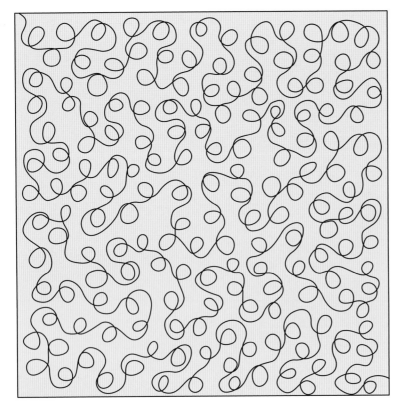

Fig. 10

Fig. 11

Variations on Traditional Stipple Quilting

On the second filler practice sample (prepare this the same as the first practice sample), try these variations (fig. 9, page 67). Trace over my designs first to understand the order and the shape to be made. Try drawing them freehand on paper next. You are now ready to try these on another practice sample.

Loopy Stipple

These look like loops, sometimes referred to as *e's* and *o's* (fig 10, top left).

Shells

Start with a small teardrop, outlining from side to side three to four times. These look nice if they go in many directions (fig. 11, bottom left).

Spiral Flowers

Make a spiral and then spiral out. Continue with one wavy line and then another wavy line (fig. 12, right).

Fig. 12

Structured Stipple

This looks like ribbon candy to me. Create these little curves in rows that go opposite directions. The second row goes in the opposite direction to look like a checkerboard (fig. 13, right).

The border design on TEA AT TENBY uses structured stippling in the ribbon candy-style to fill in small areas in an interesting way (figs. 14 and 15, page 70).

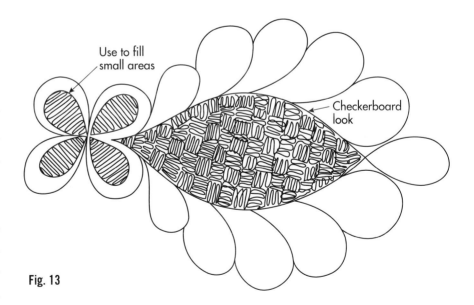

Use to fill small areas

Checkerboard look

Fig. 13

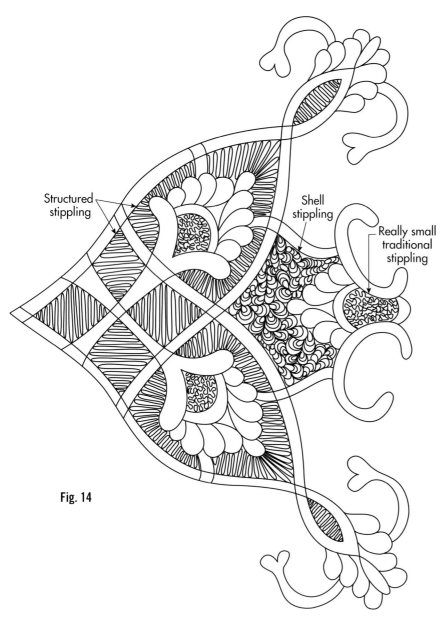

Structured
stippling

Shell
stippling

Really small
traditional
stippling

Fig. 14

above: **Fig. 14.** TEA AT TENBY border uses structured stippling, shell stippling, and small traditional stippling.

right: **Fig. 15.** Detail of the border TEA AT TENBY structured stippling

Echo Quilting

I like to echo quilt traditional feathers. This echo can be done one time or multiple times, depending on the effect you want to achieve. To echo quilt, you use quilting lines to repeat the shape of the feather (or other motifs). The stitching is spaced about ¼" from the feather. This can be done multiple times. Try to keep the distance consistent. The lines of echo quilting are not marked. Judge the distance from the feather or previous echo stitching by using the darning foot as a distance guide.

Fig. 16. An open-toe darning foot can also be used to echo.

A closed-toe symmetrical darning foot is ideal. You can follow the edge of the darning foot along the design, bumping along. I compare this to bumper cars at an amusement park. I guide my foot along the edge of the feather and when I bump into the next feather, it is time move along. Because I am using the edge of my darning foot as my guide, I can go in any direction easily.

Try echoing your practice feathers (fig. 17). It is an exclamation mark around your feather and can make it look even more beautiful!

Fig. 17. Echo quilting feathers

Crosshatching

This can be a nice choice to use as filler. Mark the area using a ruler. The size of the area will determine how far apart to mark the lines. Free-motion quilt these straight lines (fig. 18). Re-stitch to continue to the next straight line.

Crosshatching is a nice alternative filler and has a traditional appeal (fig. 19). The Project Six quilt LEMON SORBET uses crosshatching as filler (fig. 20). The crosshatch lines are marked every ¼". This project has echo quilting surrounding the feathers. The re-stitching is done along the echo stitching.

I hope you have enjoyed using stipple quilting and these creative variations as fillers for your projects. It is easier than you think to create beautiful dimension for your quilts! Next, we will learn how to quilt the actual quilt from start to finish.

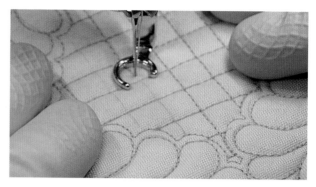

Fig. 18. Echo stitching

Fig. 19. Crosshatching stitching order:
Feather stitching in black
Echo stitching in green
Crosshatching in dark orange with re-stitching

left: Fig. 20. PROJECT SIX: LEMON SORBET and detail featuring crosshatching

opposite: Machine quilting sample using different fillers

FABULOUS Feathers & Fillers Design & Machine-quilting techniques ◆ Sue Nickels

SECTION FIVE:

Quilting the Quilt – Start to Finish

We will cover fabric selection, marking, basting, successful quilting on the home sewing machine, and finishing the quilt.

Fabric Selection

Success with your feather-quilting project starts with fabric selection. The projects featured in this book are made using 100% cotton fabric. It is important to choose a fabric for the quilt top that will show the feathers when stitched. Using solids or tone-on-tone fabrics are a good choice. Even when a matching color thread is used for the stitching, the feathers show up nicely. After all the hard work of stitching beautiful feathers, we want to be able to see them (fig. 1).

The backing fabric choice is also very important. Using a busy print that has the same colors used in the quilt top is very helpful (fig. 2). This will allow you to use the same color thread top and bobbin which will make achieving good thread tension easier.

Never use a high-contrast color of top thread versus bobbin thread. The nature of free-motion quilting with side-to-side and forward-to-backward movement of the quilt makes it hard to achieve perfect tension at all times. If the thread contrasts top and bobbin, sometimes bobbin thread will show slightly on the top and sometimes the top thread will show slightly on the back. Using the same color or similar color top and bobbin makes this slight uneven tension less noticeable.

The backing fabric is cut 2" bigger on all sides than the size of the quilt top. This allows extra fabric to hold onto when quilting close to the edge of the quilt.

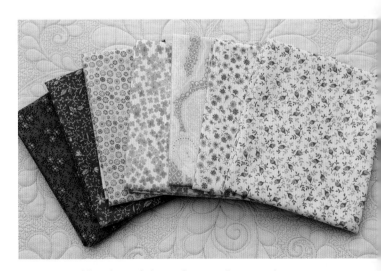

Fig. 2. Good backing fabrics for machine quilting

opposite: **Fig. 1.** Feather stitched on busy print and on solid fabric

#100 silk   60/2 cotton   50/2 cotton   50/3 cotton   40/3 cotton

FABULOUS Feathers & Fillers Design & Machine-quilting techniques ◆ Sue Nickels

Batting Selection

Review the batting information in the supplies section. Choose a batting that will give you nice results for your feather project. Cut the batting 2" bigger on all sides than the quilt top.

Thread Selection

Review the thread information in the supplies section. Choose a matching color thread to the fabric used in the quilt top. High-contrast thread color can be used once you have more experience and you have smooth and steady free-motion stitches.

The weight of the thread can also make a difference in the result you will achieve. A thinner thread will be more forgiving. A thicker and more decorative thread will show more and be less forgiving (fig. 3, page 76).

Fig. 4. PROJECT FOUR: BERRY SMOOTHIE is a good example of feathers filling the space nicely.

Deciding on Feather Designs for Your Quilt Project

Now you can design feathers to fit specific areas on your quilt. Here are some things to keep in mind for your quilt project when deciding how to quilt it. Make sure the feathers and motifs fill an area nicely. For a 12" area, don't use a small 6" feathered wreath. Use a larger feathered wreath that is proportional to the space. The whole quilt project should also be quilted evenly (fig. 4).

opposite: **Fig. 3.** Feathers and stippling stitched with different weight and color threads

Marking the Quilt Top

Marking the quilt top can take some time and needs to be done before the quilt layers are basted. It will be easier now that you know how to draw your own feathers. Refer to the supplies section for marking tools. Press the quilt top before marking because most marking tools are adversely affected by heat.

Begin by marking straight lines, using a quilters' ruler. We have learned two ways to mark feathers on our quilt project. One way is to use a center spine pattern, draw the spine directly on the fabric, then freehand draw the feathers directly on the fabric.

For the more complex wholecloth feather designs, tracing will be done. Use an original design that has been redrawn darker. Trace the design on the fabric in quadrants.

For our small quilt project, fold the quilt top in half and lightly finger-crease a line. Open the quilt top, fold in the opposite direction, and lightly finger-crease a line. Open the quilt top again and position the pattern under the quilt top, lining up the right side, bottom guidelines, and center for each quadrant. Tape can be used to prevent movement of pattern and fabric.

Make a plan and practice the free-motion stitching path to be used for this particular feather design. Use a practice piece to test the threads used in the project.

Basting the Layers

A well-basted quilt is the foundation for successful machine quilting. There are many methods available and whatever method you choose, it is important to take the time to do a good job. I have good results with safety pin basting and I am reluctant to change a good thing.

Safety Pin Basting

Cut the batting and backing 2" bigger on all sides than the quilt top. Press the backing fabric. Mark the center of each side of the top and backing, to help you align the quilt accurately. Lay the backing fabric wrong-side up on a large table (or the floor if working on a large quilt.) Tape the sides of the quilt to the table every 3" to 4". If working on a carpeted floor, use T-pins to hold the backing to the carpet. Do not stretch or distort the backing fabric. It should be smooth with no trapped fullness.

Lay the batting on the backing, smoothing out any fullness or wrinkles.

Next, place the quilt top right-side up on the batting, matching the center marks so the top and backing align evenly. Smooth the top, being careful not to stretch or pull.

On larger quilts, measure to see if the quilt is square and even. Measure side-to-side, top-to-bottom, and across the diagonals. If there is a difference, readjust the top and measure again. It is easy to distort large tops by aggressively smoothing. This is the reason I prefer laying out the complete backing, batting, and quilt top versus methods that baste in sections.

Using safety pins, start basting the center of the quilt top. Baste a cross first. Refer to figure 5, page 79. Continue basting each quadrant, as shown. Don't close the safety pins until all of them are placed. Go back and close them using a safety pin closer (See Resources, page 110). If you close the safety pins as you go it can cause some distortion of the quilt top. Place the safety pins every 3" (fig. 6, page 79). Once all the safety pins are in and closed, remove the tape or T-pins.

The last step in the basting process is to thread baste the outer edge of the quilt top to the batting and backing to neatly secure it during the quilting process. Thread baste by hand about ¼" from the edge of the quilt top with a long running stitch.

Safety pin basting is time consuming, but this is one area where saving time is not the most important issue. The secret to successful machine quilting is a well-basted quilt. Whatever method you choose for basting your quilt, do a good job. Other methods of basting include: spray-basting adhesives, thread basting, basting guns, and fusible battings. Follow the specific instructions given with the spray-basting adhesives, basting guns, and fusible battings.

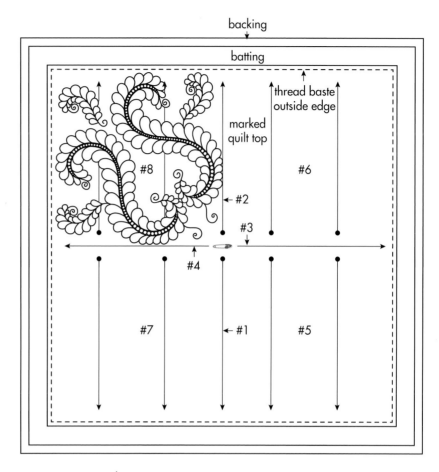

Fig. 5. Basting order

Ready to Quilt

Now the fun really begins! Let's quilt!

Refer to Supplies Section One—My Sewing Room for a review of how to arrange your sewing space for success at the home sewing machine.

Once your quilt is marked and basted, it is time to decide the order of quilting. Projects in this book don't have any straight lines.

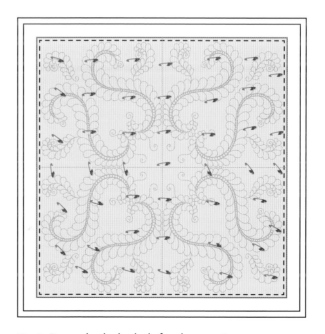

Fig. 6. Basted wholecloth feather project

Fig. 7. Wholecloth stitching order (free-motion only, no straight lines)

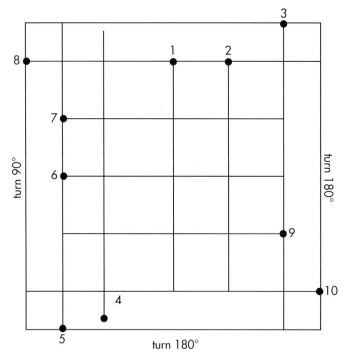

Fig. 8. Straight lines stitching order

Organize the order for working on these projects in the same way as I am describing for quilts that have marked or stitch-in-the-ditch straight lines (Fig. 7). Start with any straight lines that need to be quilted. Often on bigger projects there are straight lines in the sashing and the borders that will need to be stitched in the ditch. This is done using a walking foot with the feed dogs in place. This is important to stabilize the quilt for the rest of the process.

Determine the center-most straight line and start with that line at the top of the quilt. From the top of the quilt, sew the first straight line. Then coming back to the top, sew the next straight line directly to the right of the first line. The bulk of the quilt always moves to the left. The most there will ever be in the arm of the machine is half of the quilt or less. This makes managing a large quilt possible (fig. 7).

Once the rows are sewn to the right, turn the quilt 180 degrees or upside down. Repackage the quilt to start with the centermost line from the top down. Keep working to the right. Once you are done in this direction, turn the quilt a quarter turn, and repackage it to start with the centermost row and sew from the top down. Continue to work to the right until all straight lines are complete in that direction. Turn the quilt 180 degrees and find the centermost row. Continue to the right until all straight lines are finished (fig. 8, page 80).

Packaging the Quilt

To have good control, the quilt must be packaged properly. Lay the quilt in a large enough area to spread it out flat. Roll it evenly from each side so the rolls are a few inches from your first quilting line. Flatten the rolls to help hold them in place and to make it easier to position

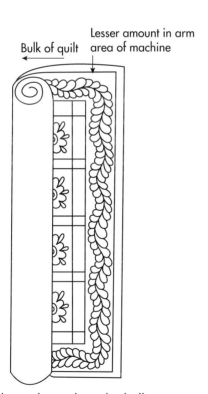

Bulk of quilt

Lesser amount in arm area of machine

Fig. 9. Package the quilt so the bulk moves to the left and the lesser amount is in the arm area of your machine.

your hands at the sewing machine. I don't use any clips to hold the rolls. Roll from the bottom to transport to sewing machine (fig. 9).

Once the straight lines are complete, begin the designs (feathers) that require free-motion quilting. Work in the same order as described for the straight lines. Find the centermost row of free-motion designs and package the quilt to sew from top to bottom. Work to the right—the bulk of the quilt moves to the left. Repackage and turn the quilt in the same order as figure 7, page 80. Once the designs are complete, begin with the fillers (stipple) that surround the designs in the same order.

The order of quilting for each quilt is different. Some quilts need to be packaged on the diagonal. Free-motion stitching on feathers is done first and the filler, such as stipple quilting, is done next. Most of the projects in this book are small quilts. Even though they are small, I still organize and package as described for larger quilts. Any pull or drag on the quilt will make it harder to have smooth and even free-motion stitching. For the smaller projects you may be able to break some of the packaging rules, but it is important to know as the quilts get bigger, you will absolutely need to follow the guidelines of proper packaging!

There is a perception that it is hard to machine quilt on the home sewing machine because of the bulk of the quilt. If the quilt is managed properly this is not true. Once you are in control of the quilt, the problems are minimal and you can achieve smooth and even stitches at all times.

Here are some tips to help you work easily no matter what size your quilt project:

◆ Rest the quilt on your chest, over your shoulder, and for large quilts use an ironing board behind you to support the weight of the quilt (fig. 10).

◆ Never let the quilt drop down in your lap.

◆ Stay as close to your machine as possible.

◆ Whenever you can't move the quilt easily, stop and reposition the quilt package.

◆ The quilt should feel as easy to move as the small quilt sandwiches used in practice.

◆ Sit straight in your chair and adjust the height of your chair to have no stress on your body.

With these techniques, you are always in control and can happily manage any size quilt.

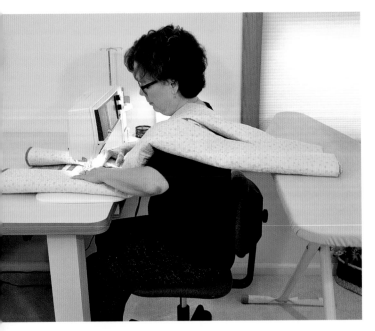

Fig. 10. Sue quilting at her machine

Finishing Your Quilt

It is time to finish your quilted project. You will need to trim the excess batting and backing from the finished quilt. Square the quilt by using a quilters' ruler, mat board, and rotary cutter. Don't trim too close to the edge of the quilt top as you will want the batting and backing to fill the binding completely. You may need to do a light blocking of the quilt, especially if it has been quilted heavily. I use a double binding cut 2¼", and for the small quilt projects have used a straight grain.

I always make a label for the quilt and attach it to the back of the quilt in the right lower corner. It should include your name, address, telephone number, size of the quilt, date the quilt was made, fabric, thread, and batting information. For quilts that will be used as wallhangings, I like to add a sleeve to the top edge. Take care when washing your quilts. I machine wash my quilts in cold water on a delicate cycle using a mild detergent. I hang my quilts to dry. Once mostly dry, I will fluff in a low heat dryer for a few minutes. Try to keep washing to a minimum.

I hope you have enjoyed learning about feathers and fillers—from design concepts to machine quilting! Remember, practice will make perfect. The more you design and stitch feathers, the easier they will become. I truly love using the concepts that are covered in this book and hope you will also. The next section includes nine wholecloth feathers. Whether you are going to design your own wholecloth project or use one of my designs, I know you will find success with the techniques you have learned from this book!

Sue Nickels

SECTION SIX:

Feather Patterns and Projects

◇◇◇

This section contains the individual feather patterns for the practice feathers discussed in Section Three: Machine Quilting Feathers. These practice samples are made using 12" squares of muslin and 12" squares of batting. You will need six 12" muslin squares and three 12" batting squares to complete the three practice exercises in the book. Have more ready as you might want to repeat some of the exercises.

Next, are the nine quilt projects featuring my wholecloth feather designs. These designs are drawn in a 6¾" square area and if they are made this size, your quilt project will be about 16" square. If you would like them to be bigger, you can enlarge the design. My finished quilts are approximately 18" squares and the designs were enlarged by 20%.

To make the 18" finished quilt size, use these yardages:

◆ **Quilt top:** ½ yard cotton fabric, or a fat quarter would work. Cut the top 18" square—use a solid or solid-like fabric.

◆ **Backing:** ⅔ yard cotton fabric. Cut the backing 22" square—use a busy print in colors to match the top fabric.

◆ **Binding:** ¼ yard. Cut 82" of 2¼" straight binding. The remaining backing fabric can be used for the binding or use a different fabric.

◆ **Batting:** 22" square cotton/poly-blend

Please note—if you adjust the size of the pattern larger than 20%, adjust the yardages accordingly.

Each wholecloth feather quilt will have the exact threads used listed with that quilt.

I hope you enjoy the quilt projects!

¼" CROSSHATCH GRID

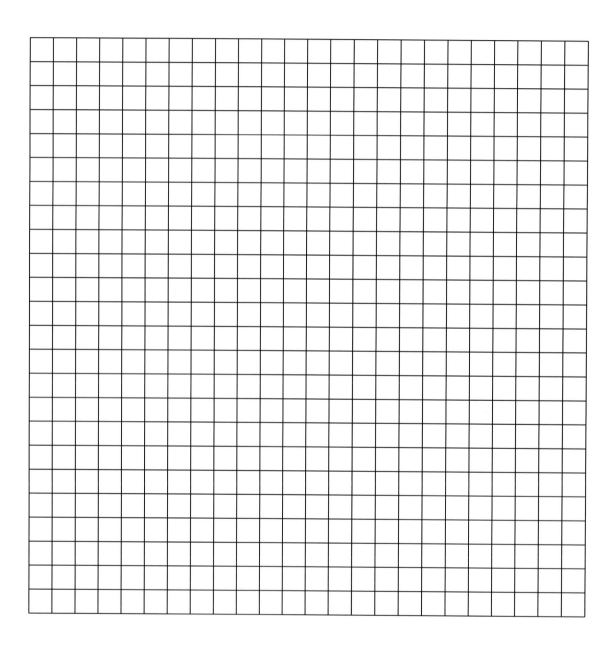

Individual Feathers: 3 SIMPLE FEATHERS

For practice feathers discussed in Section Three

FABULOUS Feathers & Fillers DESIGN & MACHINE-QUILTING TECHNIQUES ◆ Sue Nickels

Individual Feathers: FEATHERED WREATH

For practice feathers discussed in Section Three

Individual Feathers: FEATHERED PLUME

For practice feathers discussed in Section Three

Feather Projects

The nine projects that follow (pages 90–107) are drawn in a 6¾" area. The right side and bottom lines are guidelines to be used when positioning the pattern under the quilt top. These lines are *not* drawn on the fabric.

Review marking the wholecloth quilt in Section Five. Echo quilting is not marked and will not be shown on the pattern. Each pattern will have an indication of the echo quilting that has been done and how many times the feather was echoed.

Crosshatching is marked—use the ¼" grid pattern (page 84), place it under the quilt top, and mark using a ruler. When using an echo, don't mark crosshatching up to a feather; leave space for echoing.

FABULOUS Feathers & Fillers DESIGN & MACHINE-QUILTING TECHNIQUES ♦ Sue Nickels

Project One: VANILLA CREAM

17½" x 17½", made by author, 2010

Cotton fabric, 50/2 cotton thread,
    cotton/poly-blend batting
One echo, traditional stipple quilting

Project Two: MINT JULEP

17½" x 17½", made by author, 2012

Cotton fabric: Ricky Tims Rhapsody collection,
    60/2 cotton thread, 100-weight silk thread,
    cotton/poly-blend batting
Two echos, traditional and structured stipple quilting

Project Three: ORANGE SHERBET

17½" x 17½", made by author, 2012

Cotton fabric, 60/2 cotton thread,
    cotton/poly-blend batting
One echo, traditional stipple quilting

FABULOUS Feathers & Fillers Design & Machine-quilting techniques ♦ Sue Nickels

Project Four: BERRY SMOOTHIE

18" x 18", made by author, 2011

Cotton fabric, 50/2 cotton thread,
   cotton/poly-blend batting
One echo, traditional stipple quilting

FABULOUS Feathers & Fillers Design & Machine-quilting techniques ♦ Sue Nickels

Project Five: CRÈME BRULEE

17¼" x 17¼", made by author, 2012

Cotton fabric, 60/2 cotton, 100-weight silk,
    Cotton/poly-blend batting
Three echos, traditional and structured stipple quilting

FABULOUS Feathers & Fillers DESIGN & MACHINE-QUILTING TECHNIQUES ♦ Sue Nickels

Project Six: LEMON SORBET

18" x 18", made by author, 2012

Cotton fabric, 60/2 cotton thread, 100-weight silk,
Cotton/poly-blend batting
One echo, crosshatching, traditional stipple quilting

Project Seven: COTTON CANDY

18" x 18", made by author, 2012

Cotton fabric, 60/2 cotton thread,
    cotton/poly-blend batting
Two echos, traditional stipple quilting

FABULOUS Feathers & Fillers DESIGN & MACHINE-QUILTING TECHNIQUES ♦ Sue Nickels

Project Eight: WHALE PARTY

18" by 18", made by author, 2012

Cotton fabric, 60/2 cotton thread, 100-weight
silk thread, cotton/poly-blend batting
Three echos, traditional stipple quilting

FABULOUS Feathers & Fillers DESIGN & MACHINE-QUILTING TECHNIQUES ◆ Sue Nickels

Project Nine: PEACH PARFAIT

18" by 18", made by author, 2012

Cotton fabric, 60/2 cotton thread,
   cotton/poly-blend batting
Three echos, traditional stipple quilting

Bonus: TEA AT TENBY *Border Quilting Pattern*

Bibliography

These books are wonderful resources for information on machine quilting and feather designs.

Fanning, Robbie and Tony. *The Complete Book of Machine Quilting*. Radner, Pennsylvania: Chilton Needlework, 1980

Gaudynski, Diane. *Guide to Machine Quilting*. Paducah, Kentucky: American Quilter's Society, 2002

Hargrave, Harriet. *Heirloom Machine Quilting*. Lafayette, California: C & T Publishing, 1990

Holly, Pat and Sue Nickels. *Amish Patterns for Machine Quilting*. Minneola, New York: Dover Publications, Inc., 1997

Holly, Pat and Sue Nickels. *60 Machine Quilting Patterns*. Minneola, New York: Dover Publications, Inc., 1994

Lehman, Libby. *Threadplay- Mastering Machine Embroidery Techniques*. Bothell, Washington: That Patchwork Place, 1997.

Marston, Gwen and Joe Cunningham. *Quilting with Style: Principles for Great Pattern Design*. Paducah, Kentucky: American Quilter's Society, 1993.

Nickels, Sue. *Machine Quilting: A Primer of Techniques* Paducah, Kentucky: American Quilter's Society, 2003

Wagner, Debra. *Teach Yourself Machine Piecing and Machine Quilting*. Radnor, Pennsylvania: Chilton Book Company, 1992.

Resources

This is a list of products I use and I am confident of the success achieved with them. There are many other products that are available and work well, but these are the ones I have found that work the best with the techniques in this book. Most products are available at quilt shops and some are available on my website.

Tracing paper – 18" x 50 yard roll / 8.0 lb white: Utrecht Art Supplies
www.utrechtart.com

Fabric marking pencil – silver and white: Roxanne™ Quilter's Choice

Pencil sharpener: Clover® Brand

Cotton-blend batting: Hobbs Heirloom® 80/20 blend

Wool batting: Hobbs Heirloom® Washable Wool

Color fixative for commercially dyed fabrics: Retayne™ (G & K Craft Industries)

Safety pin closer: Kwik Klip™

Sewing Machine: BERNINA® 550 and 830

Mettler® cotton thread: 60/2 embroidery and 50/3 silk finish

Superior Threads:
www.superiorthreads.com

Cotton: MasterPiece™ 50/3, King Tut™ (Sue Nickels Tone-on-Tone) 40/3

Silk: Kimono™ #100

Aurifil™ Thread: cotton 50/2

YLI Thread: silk #100

Sewing Machine Needles: Schmetz Microtex sharp, sizes – 80/12 and 70/10

Easy Kut Curved tipped scissors with foam grips – Tooltron Industries
www.tooltron.com

Light Box: Gagne Porta-Trace light panel
www.gagneinc.com

To contact Sue, visit her website at
www.Sue-Nickels.com

About the Author

PHOTO: Pat Holly, Ann Arbor, Michigan

Sue has been quilting for 34 years, starting by hand and gradually focusing on machine work. She has been teaching machine techniques for the past 22 years. Sue has taught and lectured nationally for shops, guilds, and major conferences, including many times for AQS Shows. She has also taught internationally in Canada, England, Norway, Australia, New Zealand, and Spain. Sue's major awards include 1998 AQS Best of Show for THE BEATLES QUILT made by Sue and her sister, Pat Holly. Their quilt THE SPACE QUILT won the 2004 AQS Machine Workmanship Award. Sue and Pat's quilt TEA AT TENBY won 2009 Best of Show at the Birmingham Festival of Quilts in England. Sue is an AQS author and her previous books are *Machine Quilting: A Primer of Techniques* and *Stitched Raw Edge Appliqué* co-authored with Pat. Sue's priority in the workshops she teaches is to provide a relaxed environment for students to learn machine techniques that are timesaving. She emphasizes the best quality workmanship, never compromising quality for speed!

Sue lives in Ann Arbor, Michigan with her husband Tim. They have two daughters, Ashley and Jessi, son-in-law Ryan, and granddaughter Stella.

more AQS books

This is only a small selection of the books available from the American Quilter's Society. AQS books are known worldwide for timely topics, clear writing, beautiful color photos, and accurate illustrations and patterns. The following books are available from your local bookseller, quilt shop, or public library.

#8524

#8234

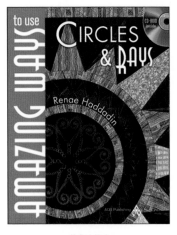

#8154

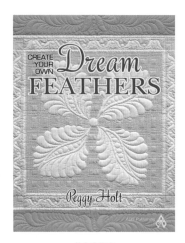

#8670

#8238

#7015

#6900